NO ROOM TO RECEIVE

Daily Affirmations of Abundance for
Living a Life of Purpose and Prosperity

ANITA D. POWELL

LifeRich Publishing is a registered trademark of The Reader's Digest Association, Inc.

LifeRich Publishing books may be ordered through booksellers or by contacting:

LifeRich Publishing
1663 Liberty Drive
Bloomington, IN 47403
www.liferichpublishing.com
844-686-9607

ISBN: 978-1-4897-4573-6 (sc)
ISBN: 978-1-4897-4574-3 (hc)
ISBN: 978-1-4897-4575-0 (e)

Library of Congress Control Number: 2022923268

Print information available on the last page.

LifeRich Publishing rev. date: 12/20/2022

Bring ye all the tithes into the storehouse, that there may be meat in mine house, and prove me now herewith, saith the Lord of hosts, if I will not open you the windows of heaven, and pour you out a blessing, that there shall not be room enough to receive it. Malachi 3:10 KJV

INTRODUCTION

It has been my blessing to share these affirmations to strengthen your daily walk and to supercharge your belief. I believe in the power that God has bestowed in our lives. I hope this work reinforces your faith to be a strong Christian warrior, and to live the abundant life God designed for you.

I thank you for investing in this book. All of the proceeds from the sale are donated to the JWP Foundation, which is a non-profit foundation dedicated to the eradication of homelessness and food insecurity in the world (think big!!). This foundation is in honor of my late younger brother, who suffered with mental illness, and lived in homelessness for many years before passing. It is a myth that those who are homeless are unloved or lazy. My brother was a vibrant, smart, humorous, and beautiful soul. I started this foundation to bless the community in his honor, and to help those who helped him along the way. I believe that as God has blessed me, it is incumbent upon me to bless others. I encourage you to engage with the Holy Word every day to tap into your spiritual energy and power. May God bless you and happy reading!

HOW TO READ THIS BOOK

This book is mostly written in first person so that the reader can practice speaking affirmation into your own life. Speaking into your life changes the way you think and act. While all the references in this book are fictional, they are representative of the daily challenges we face on our spiritual journey. Read one or two of these affirmations each day, which will prayerfully charge your strength and maximize your abundance.

The content contains four types of affirmations:

- ⇨ Affirmations in Fall – the Season New Beginnings
- ⇨ Affirmations in Winter – the Season of Cold and Death
- ⇨ Affirmations in Spring – the Season of Renewal and Growth
- ⇨ Affirmations in Summer – the Season of Light

There is also some featured content, including Daily Provoking Thoughts, Poems and Prayers. And three special inserts on <u>Your Abundant Circle</u>, <u>Financial Abundance</u> and a <u>Checklist for Wealth</u> for special considerations.

PRAYER OF AFFIRMATION

Father God, thank You for the gift of my life. Thank You for making and endowing me with the power of the Holy Spirit that guides and teaches me daily. Lord, I know You have a purpose for my life. Strengthen me each day to live up to the ordainment You have place on me, and I pray that You will provide me with the resources needed to do Your Will. Lord, each day, I seek and honor You as the Lord of my life and the author and finisher of my faith. Overflow me with courage, faith, anointing and access to positively impact the world. Thank You for abundant and eternal life that I commit back to You. Praise Father, Son, and Holy Spirit. Amen.

MY PROVOKING THOUGHT OF THE DAY

Abundance is achieved when I know the answer to these three questions:

1) What are my gifts? (What do I know how to do that I am not sure why I know how to do it?)
2) What is my purpose? (Why did God plant this gift in me, and how am I supposed to use it to glorify Him?)
3) What is my calling? (How does my gift and purpose come together to contribute to the world by serving others?)

I will reflect and meditate on these questions, and I will seek God's direction every day of my life.

TODAY'S AFFIRMATION: GETTING IN POSITION

Abundance is a gift from God, but I must do my part to receive it. I have to believe it, make room for the blessings, and get in position. Today, I will focus on getting in position by walking in integrity in all my interactions. I will stop giving my past mistakes, poor choices, and past hurt so much energy. This will leave space in my head and my heart for God to fully utilize me. I will stay focused on positive energy and surrounded by positive people. I know that negative energy is like a blood clot that builds up in some inconspicuous place in my spirit. Eventually, it begins to block the blood flow of positive energy, causing me pain and discomfort as I move through the day. I know that if I do not deal with these blood clots, I am apt to have a spiritual stroke. I clear my mind and offer myself to be fully available for God's use. This is the only way to unblock the blessings. That means I stop giving energy to my ex, who took me for granted. I stop giving energy to my longtime friend, who betrayed me. I rebuke the generational curses of drugs, alcoholism, and depression that have tried to dominate me. As I speak it today, I release it, and gain the freedom to live the abundant life I have been promised.

TODAY'S AFFIRMATION: REMOVING BOUNDARIES

I strive to live abundantly; therefore, I am not limited by only what I can see. My boundaries are not set by others' accomplishments, and my ambition is not stunted by others' failure. I have the faith and courage to follow my convictions, even without a clear roadmap. I may have a dream to be a surgeon; but, I do not know any surgeons in my family to guide or encourage me. This will not hinder my passion to follow my dreams. I believe that when God planted the vision in me, He provided the means and resources to achieve it. I may have a dream to obtain my degree; but, I do not know anyone in my circle who went to college. This will not hinder my passion to follow my dreams. I will do the research, I will reach out to a past teacher for help, or I will ask God to cross my path with someone who can inspire my passions. I may have a dream to start a business; but, I do not know anyone who has ever successfully run a business. This will not hinder my passion to follow my dreams. I will join the local chamber of commerce, seek a mentor, and take a class on writing a business plan. I will not talk myself out of a vision, because I cannot see the way. Therefore, I walk in faith, and not by sight.

TODAY'S AFFIRMATION: RECEIVING LOVE

As an abundant lover, I am mastering the art of receiving love. I know how to give it, that comes naturally to me. However, I am not yet comfortable knowing how to receive it. I block my abundance when I am closed off to others' attempts to show me how much they care.

Someone volunteering to help me is an attempt at love. I receive that today. I do not just keep saying, "No, thank you."

Someone complimenting the way I look is an attempt at love. I receive that today and will not qualify it with, "Oh, it is just an old suit I have had for years."

My boss telling me that I can kick off; although, I know I will owe him later, is an attempt at love. I receive that today and am shutting down this computer and leaving quickly before he comes back.

Life sends us messages of love every day, and I am going to stay tuned into the frequency of receiving them. I deserve every affirmation sent my way.

TODAY'S AFFIRMATION: EMBRACING OPPORTUNITIES

To live a life of prosperity, I must embrace the doors that are opened for me. I know that doors are just opportunities that will open in my life. Some of these doors will enable me to walk into my destiny, live in abundance, and to influence the world. How do I know which doors are for me? How do I know the choices God wants me to make? I believe if God does not want something or someone for me, He will close the door or will not permit it to open. By implication, the ones He leaves open, He gives me a choice to pursue. When I pursue them, the opportunities stay open for me in the season God can use it to grow and develop me. However, there are times that God needs to elevate me, and may close a door that was once open to motivate me to advance to the next season of my transformation.

Therefore, I rejoice for the job I did not get, as it holds promise for an elevated opportunity. I rejoice for the relationship I lost, as it holds promise for an elevated union. I rejoice when I am turned down for a business deal, as it holds promise for a more lucrative opportunity. I know that embracing this concept permits me to live every day in gratitude.

MY PROVOKING THOUGHT OF THE DAY

As I look back over my life, I realize that every time I was rejected, I was actually being redirected to something better.
—Steve Maraboli

What if we reimagined failure? On life's journey, we will take tiny steps, giant steps, left steps, back steps, and missteps. However, all steps mean we are trying to live our best life. Standing still and not taking chances may guarantee the lack of rejection; however, it also guarantees the lack of direction. Trust the process and walk boldly!

TODAY'S AFFIRMATION: MEEKNESS AND HUMILITY

I know the meek will inherit the earth. I also know that we are born without spirit of timidity. These concepts do not conflict. Meekness and humility are not about positioning myself as less than someone else. I am the head and not the tail.

However, I am also designed to live with spiritual confidence. Spiritual confidence is the confidence in knowing that I can do and be all things through Christ. Meekness and humility are just about who gets the credit.

This is the difference between spiritual confidence and arrogance. An arrogant person believes their blessings are based on themselves; but, a spiritually confident person believes that blessings are from the grace of God. So, I am meek and humble while also walking with my head up in the confidence that God always has my back. I also realize that meekness is not a personality type; it is not determined by the tone of my voice; and it not determined on whether I am shy. Meekness is not a behavior; it is a belief that God gets the credit for the source of my abundance.

TODAY'S AFFIRMATION: TRUSTING THE PROVIDER

As I prepare myself for work this morning, I am grateful that God has provided me with a job to feed my family and to keep a roof over my head. It may not be a perfect job; but, I express gratitude for the opportunity that is denied to so many who may be looking for work. I am also mindful that I will never let my job (the provision) become more important than God (the Provider). I keep my job and career in its proper place; I am grateful for it, but I do not allow it to steal my joy, cause me stress, affect my health, or interrupt the relationships that are the most important to my life. I realize that my job is not my calling, but it is a mechanism to express my calling. My loyalty is to the calling, and not to the job. While I will respect my boss's position, I will not allow my boss to have power over me or to steal my joy, regardless of how difficult they are to work with. Even though I cannot stand my nosy coworker, who is always watching how long everyone is on break to tattle to the supervisor, I will not risk my livelihood by tripping her down the aisle way when I see her today. I will give my best effort because I am self-motivated, even when it is not recognized by others. I do not cede my power to anyone at work; therefore, I experience abundance and prosperity at my job.

MY PROVOKING THOUGHT OF THE DAY

You are the person

who could make a difference in who I am,

who could lift my spirits and bring me joy,

who could feed me positivity,

who could invest and believe in me,

who could protect and provide for me,

who could encourage me on my worst days,

who could celebrate me on my best days,

who could change my entire life.

You are me!

TODAY'S AFFIRMATION: NO HOARDING

As a lover of my abundant life, I do not hoard. I allow the gifts God gives to make room for me. I use these gifts to make a life for my family and myself. However, I recognize that to whom much is given, much is also required.

As I am blessed with an overflow of time, I do not hoard it. I volunteer to help the needy, instead of sitting at home binge watching movies. As I am blessed with money, I do not hoard it. I take care of my family and my responsibilities, and I donate my overflow to help those who are the least of these. As I am blessed with health and well-being, I do not hoard it. I share my healthy spirit and mind to encourage others to live a healthier lifestyle. As I am blessed with positive energy, I do not hoard it. I share compliments, confidence, and good will to those I meet today.

I realize that I may run into someone today on their worst day. The positive energy I share could make the difference in how they view themselves and their path. I know that hoarding is a selfish impulse and I reject it as an abundant contributor to the world.

MY PROVOKING THOUGHT OF THE DAY

Every negative experience holds the seed of transformation.
- Alan Cohen

We are surrounded by all the negative implications of this world in which we live. We are surrounded by the life-changing experiences associated with COVID, poverty, helplessness, crime, and other world tragedies. We are also surrounded by opportunities to make a difference.

The opportunity to remember that we are more bound by what makes us similar, than what makes us different.

The opportunity to be kind and compassionate to a complete stranger.

The opportunity to be generous and grateful in the midst of chaos.

And the opportunity to practice the power of positivity and prayer.

I will stay encouraged ... this too shall pass!

TODAY'S AFFIRMATION: LEARNING WHO I AM

For the next week, I am going to spend every day reflecting on who I am, and who God made me to be. I am then going to redirect my energy to filling in the delta between the two.

How do I know who God made me to be? I am going to ask God to reveal it through reflection, prayer and heavenly conversation. I am going to fervently seek it though the intimacy of my relationship with God, and I will trust that the answers will come. I am then going to enjoy the journey that God taking me through as He builds my confidence, my wisdom, and increases my portion.

I know the closer I get to God's will for my life, the more abundant I become. It is not about God giving me more things, but it is about Him continually revealing to me what He has already given me. The closer I get to God, the more my confidence His power grows. I am then more ambitious about what I can offer to the world. The closer I get to God, the more spiritual swag I gain. Not because I am so good, but because He is Great!

PRAYER OF GRATITUDE

Lord, today, I come before You, not asking of anything, but thankful
for everything. Thank You for making me, molding me, and planting
in me seeds of greatness. Thank You for healing me, protecting me,
and providing for me and my family. Thank You for grace and mercy,
and thank You for allowing me to live in prosperity and peace, despite
my past wrongs. Thank You for releasing me from the pain of those
who have wronged me, and thank You for planting forgiveness in my
heart. Thank You for the promise to provide all my needs, according
to Your riches in glory. Thank You for your permissive will to learn,
grow and make choices in my life. Thank You for the complete
freedom that You will always be there for me. In Jesus's Name, Amen

TODAY'S AFFIRMATION: REDEFINING LOYALTY

Good morning me! In today's affirmation, I am letting go. I realize to live the abundant life I have been promised, I have to redefine loyalty. I have spent too much time being loyal to something or someone who did not reciprocate. After sitting at this job for twenty years, their return loyalty involves a layoff notice, three months of severance, and an escort out of the building by Human Resources. After sitting in this marriage for twenty years, my spouse decided she wanted excitement (with someone else). After doing everything I can for my family, not one of them showed up when things got rough for me. Enough of that! I realize that one-sided loyalty is not abundant living.

> I must let go of something old and dying, to permit
> space for something new and beautiful to grow.

A great new relationship cannot grow, when I am tethered to the old mediocre one. A new career cannot flourish, when I am stuck at this old unproductive one. A bountiful harvest cannot grow in dead soil. I intend to maximize my abundant life, and I will not waste another day accepting less than the life I deserve.

TODAY'S AFFIRMATION: FINDING THE FIT

I am a powerful, spiritually abundant soul. I am in tune with my spirit and reflective of my interactions. Today, I am listening for those things in my life that do not fit. I do not covet, tolerate, or invest in anything or anyone that does not fit me. I recognize that most of my life frustrations come from trying to force what does not fit.

I may desire to have a person in my life; however, they do not fit if they drain my energy. A fit for me is a person who inspires me, believes in me, and pours into me as much as I pour into them.

I may enjoy the money this job pays me; but it does not fit if it makes me feel less than valued. A fit for me is a position that engages me, sages me and assuages me.

I may like how good this opportunity looks on the outside; but it does not fit if it requires me to compromise my integrity. A fit for me is an opportunity to provide God the glory and let my light shine. I am listening to my energy, and I will let it guide me to the favor that fits.

TODAY'S AFFIRMATION: I AM NOT A VICTIM

I live in abundance, which means that I do not whine. I am going to have some bad days; but, I am not a victim. Life is dynamic and full of disappointments and disruptions; but, I am stronger than a few distractions. I live in gratitude for the power God granted me to make decisions, change my mind, and to expect greater. Making a bunch of noise about stress at my job does not make the job any better; maybe I will make a different choice. Whining at how much trouble my friend causes is powerless; maybe I will just change friends or change my perspective. Telling everyone who will listen how hard my life is assumes that others do not have a hard life also. Literally, everyone is struggling with something; but, I will not consistently broadcast and spread negative vibes. As bad as my day was at work today, someone else does not have a job. Even though my car broke down today, I have the money to get it fixed and someone else is walking. Yes, my hair is thinning and graying due to aging; but, someone else's hair is thinning and graying due to a chronic disease. I live in gratitude that things could be worse; therefore, I choose to see my life through the perspective of abundance and not lack.

I DID THAT TODAY!

I did that today! My abundant mindset enabled me to make bold choices today … and it felt good.

I was not intimidated by my boss's commands today; I did not give my power away … and it felt good.

I was not distracted by my spouse's discontented spirit today … and it felt good.

I was not swayed by disappointing news; I just expect better news tomorrow … and it felt good.

I did not put my dreams on hold, regardless of my father's disapproval … and it felt good.

I did not shift my mood because my friends disserted me today; I enjoyed my own company … and it felt good.

I did not waste energy with my negative Nelly coworker … and it felt good.

I am undeterred … and it feels good.

YOU CAN'T LOVE ME

You can't love me, if you do not understand my calling …

My moves will intrigue, but frustrate you,
unless you understand my calling …

My passion and resolve will intimidate you,
unless you understand my calling …

My courage and rejection of criticism will annoy
you, until you understand my calling …

My determination to execute my purpose will exasperate
you, until you understand my calling …

You can't understand my calling, unless and
until you understand your own …

Then we can fall in love.

TODAY'S AFFIRMATION: THE GOSSIPING DISTRACTION

I am powerful, strong, and fearless. Gossiping and other petty behavior is beneath me. I am too focused on my own growth and capability to offer something to the world. I do not waste time pontificating about someone else's life. I do not gossip because I do not judge others' situations. I am mature enough to know that unless I am directly involved, I do not know the entire story. Gossiping is a distraction from the accountability I owe my own life, my own calling, and my own responsibilities.

I will immediately retreat when gossip begins. I am a whole and full person. The precious time God has given me today, I will not waste it on nonsense; even if I must silence my phone for the rest of the night. The more abundantly I think, the more discriminating of my friends I become. Friends that only offer gossip and other petty conversation are becoming scarce; but, those who offer encouragement, wisdom, reflection, jokes, and red wine are welcomed!

TODAY'S AFFIRMATION: TRYING NOT TO TRY

I am an abundant thinker with a full and powerful mind. I try not to use the word "try." I know that it is a useless term fraught with escape hatches that gives me an out to real commitment. I throw that word away to enable my abundance. It is a word of a lazy mind that gives me a safety net for expected failure, and provides an excuse for lacking dedication and commitment.

I am not going to try to have a good day; I have decided to have one.
I am not going to try to lose ten pounds; I am
putting the butter pecan ice cream back!
I am not going to try to be a better dad; I am going to
help my son with his homework after school.
I am not going to try to be a better Christian;
I am going to Bible study tonight.
I am not going to try to control my temper; I am going
to stop cussing out my neighbors when I get mad.
I can do all things, big and small, through Christ who strengthens me.

TODAY'S AFFIRMATION: LIFE IS TOO SHORT

I think abundantly, which means I view life through a positive lens. I expect the best in people, because I know that we are not to be judged by our worst day. But I also protect my energy and spirit from negative, brash, and disrespectful people. I do not condone, support, or provide access to anyone who consistently interjects divisiveness into my life. Although I wish and want to see the best in others, I know that many people are wearing a fake smile and a fake disposition. As an abundant thinker, I am willing to share my spirit with anyone who is receptive; but, I am a good steward of my heart, mind, body, and spirit.

I recognize that a person is who they really are under stress. A person is kind, caring and considerate on Monday, but when something goes wrong at work, they turn despondent and depressed or angry and bite me - well, that is who they really are. I do not waste my life counting the times the person was good, and the times when they were bad. I believe the consistently bad times and move on. Life is too short!

TODAY'S AFFIRMATION: PUTTING THE PAST AWAY

To live the abundant life I desire, I have to put my past in perspective. I recognize the role my past plays. It provides experiences for my growth, perspective on my path, and a testimony. However, I am not nostalgic and do not ride on my past as the upper limit of my future. Riding on past accomplishments restricts growth, building on them creates possibilities.

I have heard my best days are ahead of me, which I believe and act on every day. I refuse to believe that my life climaxed by something I did ten years ago. I also do not seek to relive my past or live in regret. I am thankful that God provides multiple opportunities in my life, and one missed moment or closed door does not stop my future prosperity. I should have focused more on school, but that does not set a lower limit for me; I can always go back. I should have accepted that sports scholarship, but that is not the bottom of my life; God opened another door for me to teach. I should not have left that relationship, but God prepared a better companion for me today. Living in the past blocks my life for today and hope for tomorrow

MY PROVOKING THOUGHT OF THE DAY

Never turn down your ambition because someone
else is uncomfortable with the volume.
-Joubert Botha

Ambition is not a dirty word! It is a strong desire to do or achieve
something that typically requires determination and hard work.
Ambition fuels my contribution. So, I will start that business I have
always wanted to; I will turn that hobby into my passion; I will go for
that new job or promotion I have worked; or I will mentor someone I
don't have to. I will offer my time, unique talents, and wisdom to the
world. I will live my life at its' highest volume. It is what I was made for!

TODAY'S AFFIRMATION: MAKING A CONTRIBUTION

I do not show up empty handed. As an abundant citizen of the world, I am a mature contributor to my life. I do not expect my relationship, my organization, my family, or my job to provide me with something that I cannot offer. I realize that anything I am a part of cannot be greater than the sum of its parts, if I do not show up as a whole contributor.

I do not ask for something from a relationship
that I am not willing to give.
I do not expect my company or job to run smoothly if I do not.
I do not expect my family to have joy and peace if I do not.

When I am bringing my best, only then can I expect more from others. I believe that excellence and abundance are contagious; so, I demonstrate that today. I will offer this to the world, but I will not accept anything less than what I deserve in return.

DESPITE THE PAIN

It has taken all my positive energy to address my own shortcomings and deal with the pain of my past.

It has taken fervent prayer to live a positive life of intention, despite the pain of loss.

It has taken conviction to live in power and praise, despite the pain of abuse.

It has taken courage to thrive in my purpose, despite the pain of rejection.

It has taken faith to live as a healthy individual, despite the pain of criticism and negativity.

It has taken belief in what God gifted me to have confidence and credence, despite the pain of failure and defeat.

Despite the pain, I am determined to let it go and live the abundant life God promised me.

I do not carry my pain … and I cannot carry yours.

TODAY'S AFFIRMATION: RICHER RELATIONSHIPS

It may seem counterintuitive, but the more abundant my life becomes, the less people there are around me. However, the less people in my life, the richer my relationships become. My quality of relationships become more important than the quantity of people in my life. My destiny is ordained by God. I am fully aware that while some people may not be able to help me on the road to my destiny, most can hurt me.

People who obviously wish me ill are not that dangerous; I see them coming and can predict their moves. However, I am on the lookout for those in my life who just tolerate my calling. They may not overtly discourage me; but, they will not help me. They do not deny me; but, they will not invest in me. I am wary of anyone who can watch me struggle with my destiny, have the ability to help me, but does not have the desire.

I am thankful to God for exposing those in my life who are not really for me. I am thankful to God for pruning those who poison my vision. I am thankful to God for elevating those who work for my good.

TODAY'S AFFIRMATION: SELF-MOTIVATED

I am an unstoppable force, and I am self-motivated to be my best. While I am grateful if someone else recognizes and acknowledges how awesome I am, I do not need this recognition. I am an abundant resident on this Earth, and I am motivated with same high level of work ethic in whatever I do. It does not matter if I am doing a volunteer effort for no pay, or making lots of money. I focus on what I can control … my input. The output takes care of itself, because I believe I will reap what I sow. Therefore, I sow at a very high level, and I expectedly wait to reap what God is sending my way.

I am not waiting for things to be perfect for me to offer my best. It may not be the optimal job I want; but, I will offer my best until that opportunity opens. It is not the dream house I want; but, I will take the best care of my apartment until that chance comes along. It is not the car I really want; but, I will wash it, put in the good gas, keep the tires rotated, and pay the car note on time until the one I want is available. I know the way I show up now determines the opportunities to come; so, I do not wait for joy, peace, and success before I give my best.

TODAY'S AFFIRMATION: MEANING OVER STABILITY

I know and welcome that an abundant life is dynamic and engaging. I know and accept that my life will be full of twists and turns, hurdles and humps, luxuries and loneliness, and winters and warmness; but, I would not have it any other way. I strive for my life to have meaning instead of stability.

I do not expect my family and friends, my job, boss or coworkers, my children, my home, or my station in life to provide me stability. I do not put my hope or joy or expected blessings in the hands of others. I am a fully engaged partner with God in my life's journey, showing up to do His Will. I am committed to spreading joy, comforting, and helping others as He has commanded. My expectations for the abundant life I deserve comes through the promises He made, that only He can fulfill. As I embrace this concept, I do not live a life of disappointment. I look for the best in others, but do not rely on it for my happiness. I pray for the peace in my family, but do not count on it before I can move forward. I inspire excellence in those around me, but do not lean on them for returned support. The source of my stability is in Christ alone!

TODAY'S AFFIRMATION: BELIEVING GOD

I know that the first part of an abundant journey is belief in God. However, belief in God alone is insufficient to experience life's abundance; I know that I must also believe God. I realize that my abundant life will never materialize if I do not believe God's promise:

that I am the head and not the tail,
that He knows the plans He has to prosper me,
that He did not build me with a spirit of fear,
that His abounded grace will prosper me in all good works,
that He will overflow me so there will not be room enough to receive,

Instead of the negative self-talk, I speak these words of faith. I will think, speak, act, and make decisions based my belief in God's image of me. This is the belief that brings me joy and positions me to make a difference in the world!

TODAY'S AFFIRMATION: THE CUMULATIVE EFFECT

As an abundant spirit, I think and dream big. I know I have the capacity for a big impact; so, I do not shy away from it. However, I am equally aware that small steps can also add up to something huge. While I am expectedly waiting for the big dream, I am not sitting on the couch watching internet TV, waiting on God. The smallest steps sometimes unlock the opportunity for the bigger ones.

I manifest my faith by demonstrating that I believe in His promises and deliverance. While I am waiting for God to increase my new business, I show my measure of faith by doing research to gain more knowledge and registering my business name. While I know that God will send a new relationship my way, I am meditating and clearing my mind of past hurt and abuse so that I do not impose this onto my new relationship (and doing sit-ups.) While I am praying to God to deliver me a son, I am cleaning out the guest room and preparing a place for my son to live. I believe in abundance; therefore, I expect and prepare for the blessing!

TODAY'S AFFIRMATION: LIVING FOR THE WEEKEND

Living for the weekend is a very popular mantra. I know the saying is meant to convey a sense of relief that the weekend is coming, and the sense of joy I will have when I am free from work. It is mostly harmless. However, as an abundant thinker, I am aware of how powerful both my thoughts and words are to the engine that drives my life. Living for the weekend implies that my happiness is conditional on Friday night. Conversely, I sometimes experience Sunday blues when it is time to prepare for work the next day.

I live abundantly; therefore, think differently than others. I live for and enjoy every day of my life. I do not wait for Saturday to laugh or cry; I do it on Tuesday morning. I eat crab legs on Thursday after work. I go out with friends to the movies on Sunday night. I stay up late to comfort a good friend on Wednesday night. I know that every day God wakes me is another day I get to make a difference, to experience joy, and to express my calling. So, Monday brings me as much joy as does Saturday. I speak it, think it, and live it. I then watch the fruits of my labor, my resources, and my impact grow to overflow!

TODAY'S AFFIRMATION: GIVING AND GROWING

Good is the enemy of great! I realize that contentment and ambition can co-exist. I rebuke anyone for making me feel as if I should not pursue the greater, because I have the good. I am grateful every day for my life and the opportunity to live it. I also recognize that every day God gives me breath is a day to offer something unique and wonderful to the world. I do not believe that where I am and what I have is good enough. This is not a negative expression of my life, and it is not about being less than enough. This is an expression that I always have more to give. When I stop giving and growing, there is no point to my existence.

When I stop striving after I achieve a good outcome, I never get to a great one. When I settle into a good job, I never see the opportunities for a great one. When I accept only the things I can see, I nullify the ultimate place of greatness that God has destined for my life. If I am content with just good enough, I will never know how awesome I am made to be. As I am convicted by the energy inside me to do and be more, there is more to do and be.

BOOK INSERT ABUNDANT LIFE ASSESSMENT WHO IS IN YOUR CIRCLE?

Abundant people are not abundant alone. While we are not defined by those closest to us, we are influenced by them. We have heard the adage that we are average of the five people closest to us. So, what does that make me and you, if we are constantly surrounded by those who are not living abundantly, those who are not striving and seeking a prosperous life, and those who are not walking in their purpose. Take this quick circle of friends' assessment to evaluate whether it is time to level up the quality of those associations around you.

WHO SHOULD BE IN YOUR CIRCLE OF INFLUENCE? TRUE FRIENDS

_____ True friends recognize, honor, and value your gift. They will support (and push you, as needed) toward your greatest potential. A true friend will never let you settle into mediocrity.

_____ True friends are also seeking God first and walking in their own gift. Otherwise, they will not understand or value your moves and decisions. Those who also on the path to their own destiny will respect yours.

_____ True friends do not criticize you. Criticizing someone is just pointing out everything you do wrong. This is an envious spirit. Someone who truly loves you will give you honest feedback, but will also offer to help you improve. A true friend invests in you to realize your dreams.

_____ True friends keep your secrets; but they will also challenge you to be your best self without judgement. If you make a mistake, love will compel them to help you recover. True friends do not think themselves superior to you.

WHO SHOULD BE IN YOUR CIRCLE OF INFLUENCE? REAL FRIENDS

_____ Real friends do not mock or downplay your dreams. True love understands that we all have a purpose. A valuable member of your circle will help you seek and discover that purpose, as opposed to tolerating, placating, or denigrating it.

_____Real friends speak positivity into your life. They do not just pray for you, but will pray with you in seasons of challenges. Those who truly love you want the best for you and will not compete with you; but, they will always celebrate and honor you.

_____ Real friends believe in you, even when you do not believe in yourself. Real friends will stand in the gap of your doubt, cover and be an intercessor when your faith begins to wane. When you cannot stand alone, God will honor your friends' faith and send a blessing based on their love.

_____ God has a permissive will; therefore, He will often permit someone in your life, of your choice. However, real friends are those sent by God. How do you know the difference? Keep reading …

WHO SHOULD BE IN YOUR CIRCLE OF INFLUENCE? GODLY FRIENDS

Sign #1: Your spirits align: God tells us that where a few come together, He will be in the midst. For those you consistently spend time, God's presence in your interactions will be evident. The Holy Spirit inside each of you will facilitate the dialogue and you will feel refreshed, motivated, and affirmed by your interactions. If you constantly feel drained, despondent, and dispirited in their presence, this is not a Godly friend.

Sign #2: Understanding is effortless: You do not have to learn how to communicate with a friend sent by God. God is not the author of confusion; therefore, a fellowship that is ordained is facilitated by God in a trusting space. If you constantly feel as if your friend "just does not get you," they are not a Godly friend.

Sign #3: Have a role in your purpose: God created us each with a purpose for His glory and edification. Anyone He intentionally places in your life has a role in that purpose. Godly friends will serve to push you closer to your purpose. If you feel as if your friend disparages, distracts, or discourages your purpose, they are not a Godly friend.

PRAYER OF DISCERNMENT

Lord, thank You for the gift of fellowship and friendship of those You have placed in my circle to support, guide and affirm me. I ask the Holy Spirit to continue to impart the wisdom and discernment; so, that I can determine those who have been sent to propel toward my destiny and those I have permitted to distract me. Father, remove those from my life who the enemy is using to steal, kill and destroy the visions, spirit and dreams You have placed in me. Confirm for me today who should be in my circle, and give me the strength and courage to walk away from those who are not good for me. All these things I pray, in your name. Amen.

TODAY'S AFFIRMATION: REBOUND IS INEVITABLE

I understand the concept that when the markets are down, I should invest more money. That is not the time to pull out my investment; although, it appears that my stock has devalued.

> I buy when the stock is low, because I believe
> that the rebound is inevitable.

This fundamental principle of abundance applies not only to financial management. In life management, when I am down, feel devalued, or feel that my stock has depreciated, that is not the time to sell. I invest double in myself. I lost my job, so I go back to school. My marriage ended, so I focus on directing my energy to improve myself. My house was foreclosed on, so I focus on starting over and retooling my financial health. I am physically unwell, so I begin to invest more in exercising and changing my eating habits.

> I invest in myself when I am down, because I believe
> the rebound is inevitable. I believe the rebound will
> be immeasurably more than I can ask.

TODAY'S AFFIRMATION: I WILL PROSPER

Today, I rejoice that even when I cannot see my way, I do not have to live in stress and worry. I know that God has already prepared me for prosperity and a future. Therefore, even when I am a little distressed today, I have faith that God is still working all things for my good. I can rely on this promise, although I am down, do not feel my best, and feel defeated. I am comforted and encouraged that God is always working on my behalf. I rest in comfort knowing that I do not have to figure it all out by myself.

I can trust in His Word and rely on His promises,
knowing that He still intends to prosper me:

even when I have made mistakes and poor choices;
even when I have been disobedient and have backslid;
and even when I have lost a measure of faith.

A mustard seed of faith is enough to bring me back to the place of accord with God. Not because I am good; but, because greater is He that is within me than he that is in the world.

BLESSED BEYOND MEASURE

Today I redefine wealth to not be about money or material possessions.

I am blessed with the gift of choice.
I am blessed with gift of my voice.

I am blessed with the gift of discernment.
I am blessed with the gift of fulfillment.

I am blessed with the unlimited ability to plant seeds.
I am blessed with unlimited potential to fill needs.

I am blessed with the unlimited ability to give.
I am blessed with the unlimited potential to live.

I am blessed beyond measure.

TODAY'S AFFIRMATION: NO CRITICIZING

I expect abundance in my life; therefore, I do not criticize others. I understand the courage it takes to follow my dreams, to step out on faith, and to walk the path God has laid before me. I honor and respect my path; therefore, I do not criticize others for taking their own. I am aware that my words and actions may make a difference in someone's life. Maybe the negative thing I say could discourage them from pursuing the calling God ordained for them. Maybe the positive encouragement I give could be the difference maker in their confidence to keep trying. I do not heckle a granddad of three who decided to follow his dream to become a comedian, although his jokes were not that funny. I do not discourage a GED student from applying to college, just because it may be harder to get accepted. I do not discourage a friend from starting a business, reminding them every day that most businesses fail. I realize that criticism is a tool of the enemy that can push someone into doubt. I will not let the enemy use me to distract, delay or discourage someone else's path. I believe I can do all things through Christ who strengthens me; therefore, others can also.

TODAY'S AFFIRMATION: FREEDOM

Today, I challenge the traditional notions of abundance. I redefine abundance from being about what I have, what I can get, what I do, and what I make, to be only about freedom. Abundance is freedom. By God's promises, I am free from my past bad choices. I am free from disappointments and discouragement from those who were supposed to love me. I am free from oppression from those who want to harm me. I am free of the need and reliance on material possessions, status, or the need for importance. I am free from bad relationships and missed chances. I am free from stress and worry, caused by a difficult boss or overwhelming job. My abundant life lets me release the pain, stress, worry, and negativity that Jesus took to the cross. By knowing that He has already paid for me, I can live my life unencumbered with what others think of me, and what society says I should do or be. I do not have to trying to keep up with the Jones (or Jacksons, or Garcias or Nguyens or Smiths). I am free to pursue the passions and desires God has placed in my heart. I am free to live in joy that fills my spirit. I am free to have peace every day, despite the negativity that may surround me. I finally get it; abundance is my state of mind!

ENDINGS ARE NEW BEGINNINGS

As I strive to live an abundant life, I do not fear endings. I know that only in endings can a new beginning arise. Endings are a natural part of life; so, I do not stress over them. I have reshaped my perspective that when I experience an ending, I expect the new beginning that is ordained to follow. This does not mean that all endings are good to me; but, I know that endings are good for me.

> The end of my marriage means a new opportunity for love.
> The end of my college days means a new
> opportunity for a professional career.
> The end of my job means a new opportunity for promotion.
> Retirement means a new opportunity to pursue my passion.

I do not worry or stress about endings today. I am in expectation for the new beginning to come.

TODAY'S AFFIRMATION: STAYING ENCOURAGED

As I strive to live an abundant life, I do not believe statistics. If I pay attention to the statistics, I will get discouraged and lose my faith. I believe in God's promises and if He ordained it, there is 100 percent of success.

I do not care that most new small businesses fail in the first
ten years; God has ordained mine, so I will succeed.
I do not care that half of marriages end in divorce;
God has ordained mine, so it will last.
I do not care that only one person out of the ten of us who applied
will get the promotion; God has ordained it, so I will receive it.

It may not look the way I expect and may not come on the timing I have defined; but, it is already mine. I do not accept that failure is a real thing; it is an imaginary construct created by the enemy to keep me afraid to try. Therefore, I will continue to pursue what has been placed in my spirit, and I will not give up prematurely. I will not give up because I have decided I have failed, or because others around me have told me it too hard. I believe in the impossible because faith is a crazy thing!

TODAY'S AFFIRMATION: TRUSTING MY ENERGY

As a person who lives abundantly, I am in tune with my energy. I vibrate on a frequency of positivity, love, and giving, and I manifest these traits into my life. I have learned that my energy does not lie. Even if my eyes cannot see it, my energy can feel toxicity.

My energy will monitor when I am constantly
around someone who drains my life force.
My energy will validate who is not good for me.
My energy will affirm whether I should accept the job or keep looking.
My energy will warn me when I need to rest and recharge.
My energy will send an alert when something
is out of balance in my body.

My energy does not lie. I will not ignore my energy, even when it does not seem logical. I recognize that my energy is a gift from God, designed to protect and guide my life. I do this because I trust the energy and instincts I have been gifted and I stay tuned for direction from the Holy Spirit every day.

TODAY'S AFFIRMATION: NO HATING

As a person who strives to live an abundant life, I do not waste my time hating. To hate takes too much energy; energy which I need to engage in my own life; energy I need to be a great dad; and energy I need to be successful and follow my own calling.

Hate drains my life force, and distracts from my purpose.
Hate redirects me to the most negative experiences in my life.
Hate shackles me into the darkest places of my existence.

I know I am supposed to love my enemies (ok, I am still working on this one). However, I know it starts with releasing the anger and pain they caused. As I evolve past this anger and pain, I commit to release my instinct for vengeance and allow God to have the final say. Once I evolve beyond vengeance, I can reshape my interactions and feelings. I know that loving my enemies does not require that I continually allow them access to my heart and spirit. I can move in freedom to enjoy my abundant life without surrendering any of my power to hate.

TODAY'S AFFIRMATION: REAPING WHAT I SOW

I know that to experience an abundance of success in my own life is a function of the seeds I plant in others. I believe that I will reap what I sow; therefore…

to reap a harvest of success in my life, I commit to invest in others.
To reap a harvest of success in my life, I mentor others. To reap
an abundance of success in my life, I celebrate the success of
others and vouch for those without an expectation of return

I help those I do not have to;
I push those who need it;
I strive with and for others who need a boost;
I empathize and encourage those who are down on
their luck, and I provide an avenue of redemption
for those who have stumbled along the way.

I give because I have been given to.
I show grace because it has been shown to me.
I forgive because I have been forgiven, and
I share the seeds of promise that God has endowed in
me, and I expectedly await the harvest to come.

TODAY'S AFFIRMATION: JOY THROUGH THE RAIN

It is been a tough day today. I did not get the promotion I wanted, and my spouse and I are having tension again. Just because I strive to live abundantly, does not mean every day is a good day for me. I know that it rains on the both the just and unjust. This means that just because I walk in faith and believe God does not mean that He will always remove the rain from my life.

> But, through all the power He has given me, I can choose
> to have joy and peace even through the rain.

I live an abundant life; so, I understand that I have joy when things go well, and when they do not. Therefore, I am warm, kind, joyous and gracious when everything is coming up roses, and show the same kindness when everything is coming up thorns. Joy is not conditional on if I physically feel my best today; it is not conditional on if others treated me kindly; it is not conditional on if I got what I wanted out of life. I shine my light and build my resilience by showing the world that I still am who God says I am, even when I am down.

MY PROVOKING THOUGHT OF THE DAY

Whatever seeds I plant or allow to be planted in my heart, mind and spirit is what will produce fruit.

Planting apple seeds produces apples. It cannot produce peaches.

Planting or allowing criticism in my life produces difficulty and confusion. It cannot produce confidence.

Planting or allowing derogatory messages produces disrespect. It cannot produce prosperity.

Planting or allowing negativity in my environment or in my thoughts produces discontentment. It cannot produce gratitude.

Planting or permitting doubt in my vision produces a dream denied. It cannot produce destiny.

TODAY'S AFFIRMATION:
ABUNDANT RELATIONSHIPS

As I choose to enjoy the abundant life I have been given, I live that life with other abundant thinking people. I am fully committed to the relationship with my partner. My heart is open, and I give generously of myself to the good of the relationship. I do not hold my past hurt, betrayal, and trauma against them or close myself off to the love I and they deserve. I love, support, and encourage my partner to be their best, and I motivate my partner to discover the best version of themselves. I am considerate and kind and even when we disagree; therefore, I do not intentionally tear them down. I do not criticize their efforts to grow and develop themselves, and I engage in the relationship with the full intention to make it work. I do not take their presence and love for granted. As I offer this full measure of devotion to my partner, I know that I am worthy of reciprocity. I do not accept abuse, manipulation, or disrespect from my partner. I receive the love they offer with a full heart, and I am grateful for their efforts to show up in their best way. I communicate with intention for us to enjoy full intimacy and partnership. I know that if we both seek God first, the joy, peace and togetherness in our relationship will be added, and our relationship will be blessed.

TODAY'S AFFIRMATION:
LIVING EXCELLENTLY

In my quest to live an abundant life, today I exude excellence. Yeah, I could get by with mediocrity; certainly, everyone else does. I can give a little effort and get a C; or, I can put in a little more effort and get the B. I can do only what is required of me at work today and get by just fine; everyone else does. In fact, Chris comes to work every day, is incompetent, and doing the bare minimum; yet, he has the same job I have and makes the same amount of money. I can let this sour me on the job, or I can work to the maximum of my capability. My friends put little effort into our friendship; so, I can just adjust my effort to match theirs. Or, I can give my best in the hopes it will influence them to appreciate the relationship in a new way. As I sow seeds of excellence, extra effort, belief, tenacity, I will reap a bountiful harvest of promotion, harmony, advancement, and overflow. I do not expect my rewards to come from those I work for; however, I know that reaping of a bountiful harvest comes from God. I do not work to other's opinions or satisfaction, but I commit that my efforts to be pleasing to God's sight.

TODAY'S AFFIRMATION: DESIRING GOD

As an abundant spirit abiding on this Earth, I have desires. Sure, there are things I want for my life, for my family, and for my career. I believe that because God favors me, He will endow me with the desires of my heart. However, I do not limit my life to my desires. God has promised me that He is able to do far more abundantly than I can ask or think. This means that God will plant desires in me that I have not thought of before. God will plant desires in me that are bigger than I can see or have ever seen. God will establish visions in my spirit that are more elaborate that I could imagine on my own.

What I may want for myself is good, but what God wants for me is ...

magnificent and magnanimous,
unlimited and unequivocal,
remarkable and resounding,
and life-changing for me and those I am designed to touch.

I pray to God today to plant His desires in my heart and provision those desires to become reality.

ACCOUNTABLE LIFE

I desire to live my best life, which means I am accountable for me.

I am accountable for my decisions and choices.

I am accountable for who I permit in my life,
and who I allow to influence me.

I am accountable for how I react to things that happen to me.

I am accountable to how I show up in relationships.

I am accountable for my intentions, and how
I impact the world around me.

I am accountable for my trauma triggers and my responses to them.

I am accountable for my moods, and how I treat others.

I am accountable for my life.

TODAY'S AFFIRMATION: WALKING IN FAITH

Abundance requires a walk of faith. I do not live in fear, or let it drive my decisions. The funny thing about faith and fear is they require the same amount of belief in something that I cannot see. They are just opposites.

Fear requires me to believe the worst thing is going to happen if I try.
Faith requires me to believe the best thing is going to happen if I try.

Both can change the trajectory of my life. However, they cannot co-exist. If I live and walk in fear, I cannot simultaneously walk in faith. Therefore, if I must pick one, I opt to go with faith. Faith is the one that requires me to believe in the best possible outcome; the one that gives me courage and hope; the one that enables me to thrive, even when things do not go my way. Sure, there are times that I might feel overwhelmed, but I embrace it and take a step anyway. Sure, there are times when my confidence may wane, but I am grateful that God will send confirmation and affirmation to keep me going. I am confident that I have been equipped with the ability to climb over, punch through, or move any mountain in my way.

ABUNDANT RELATIONSHIPS REQUIRE COMPATIBILITY

Abundant relationship require compatibility.

Two good people coming together is not enough;
Two good people who are attracted to each
other coming together is not enough;
Two good people who are smart and successful
coming together is not enough;
Two good people who are God-fearing coming together is not enough;
Two good people who are attracted to each other, are smart and
successful, and who are God fearing coming together is not enough.

Abundant relationship require compatibility.

Opposites do not attract … for long.
Compromise does not last … for long.
Lack of reciprocity does not last … for long.
Being unequally yoked does not last … for long.

Abundant relationships require compatibility.

ABUNDANT RELATIONSHIPS
REQUIRE COMPATIBILITY

Spiritual compatibility: We both are seeking God first, and we accept that a healthy union is added when we do. God is the author of our lives and the facilitator of our relationship.

Intellectual compatibility: We mentally stimulate each other, and we inspire each other to follow our passions and dreams.

Emotional compatibility: We both have the emotional maturity to speak our minds, value our and each other's voices, and we can talk to each other about anything.

Sexual compatibility: We both have similar sexual interests and libido, are comfortable with each other, and we trust each other to create and maintain mutual sexual satisfaction.

World View: We have similar views about the way the world works; therefore, we can understand and dialogue on important issues without strife.

Abundant relationships require compatibility.

TODAY'S AFFIRMATION:
FINANCIAL SECURITY

As a person who practices an abundant lifestyle, I do not believe in the concept of financial security. I recognize that by using this term, I may mistakenly begin to believe that security comes from the finances (the provision), instead of from God (the Provider). I desire money and the material possessions that money allows me to enjoy, but I keep it in perspective. I do not fall in love with the money, and I will not do just anything for it. I also know that finances, just like any other resource, may change in seasons. When I am in a season of financial abundance, I am a good steward of the money I have been blessed with. I am responsible, I put some aside for the lean times, and I give to help the least of these. I also know that it is Ok to splurge on something I want, if I do not become beholden to the possession for my joy. When I experience a season of financial drought, I do not panic. I know that although my provisions have changed, my Provider has not. This too shall change. I know that everything I have lost, God will not just replace, but will overflow. Therefore, my job during times of financial drought is to trust, have faith, and to maintain my cool. A new season is coming, and it will be so prosperous that I will not have room enough to receive.

MY PROVOKING THOUGHT OF THE DAY

No more waiting …

for the right time to start this business
for the right time to be in this relationship
for the right time to go back to school
for the right time to write this song
for the right time to get my health in order
for the right time to make a stronger relationship with my children
for the right time to be honest
for the right time to get a new house
for the right time to lose weight
for the right time to help others
for the right time to make the doctor's appointment
for the right time to apply for this job
for the right time to fix this relationship with my dad
for the right time to leave this unhealthy relationship
for the right time to start this podcast
for the right time to donate my time and talents
for the right time to be happy

The right time is right now!

TODAY'S AFFIRMATION: TRIGGERING GRIEF

Even though it has been years, certain things still trigger grief over my loved one. Most days, I am good; however, today is a tough day. I live in abundance, so I want to think something positive and affirming; but I just feel sadness. I am a little mad at myself for getting off course today; I am a fierce powerhouse of awesomeness, right? But, today, that is not how I feel. Ok, I know that I cannot dull my grief and my pain; that will only suppress it. So, I need to give myself permission to deal with this today. I am not going to drink the pain away, eat it away, or smoke it away. I am going to lean in and feel it. I might cry, maybe I will curse (the hard-core words), but I need to feel this pain for it to move through me, and for it not find a home. I commit to myself that I will not sit in this pain for too long. Maybe I can find a way to turn this pain into power, by doing something my loved one cared about. Or, I can honor them with a special post, or call a mutual friend to talk about how amazing they were. It is okay to take time to grieve and recharge my batteries. I will be back in force, because I know that when God wakes me tomorrow, He has a purpose for me!

TODAY'S AFFIRMATION: LIFE TRANSITIONS

I know and accept that I will go through changes every day, big and small. I roll with those changes and understand that life is not about things happening in the order that society says it should. However, transitions are different. A life transition is a life change so big that I am different once I experience it.

This divorce has changed my view of stability and love. Retiring has changed my value proposition, without a career. Having this child has reset everything I thought was important to me. This move two states away from my parents is making me grow up quickly. I am now a new creature, and it feels exciting some days and scary others. But, I have decided to accept and welcome life transitions. They are a way for me to leap forward in growth. I have to now stretch myself into something or someone I have never been before. I know that growth comes from being uncomfortable, but if I lean into this life transition, I am guaranteed to come through it stronger and more resilient. I do not mourn who I used to be; I realize that new challenges in life bring opportunities for me to grow. It is hard, but I am going to do it anyway and watch the testimony that comes from this season.

MY PROVOKING THOUGHT OF THE DAY

If something as small as the faith of a grain of a mustard seed can impact the world, what could my fervent faith do?

If something as unseen as COVID can change the world, what could my hope do?

If something as ambiguous as love can define a nation, what could my kindness do?

If something as innocuous as a speech can change hearts and minds, what could this book do?

If something as small as a seed can grow fruit for a lifetime, what can my seed of encouragement do?

If something as small as a zygote can become a giant, what could my seed of belief become?

Something So Small ...

TODAY'S AFFIRMATION: GOING FOR IT

Life is not a trial run. I do not get a do over; I do not get a chance to look back at the end, assess what I missed and try it again. So, why do I let one more day pass me by without going for the dreams and visions that have been placed in me? Can I wake up at ninety and face the fact that I never actually tried to live the life I wanted? I will not be the person who loved someone my entire life, but never told them because I feared rejection. I will not be the person who dreamed of being an artist all my life, but I worked a 9-5 because that is what everyone told me was the safe career move. I will not be the person who had been gifted with a great idea, but never pursued it. I will not live with regret, and I will leave it all on the table. When I reflect on my life at the end, I want to tell stories of how good it felt to pursue my dreams; I want to encourage my great-grandchildren to go for it; and I want to laugh about the crazy things I tried that nobody else thought was possible. I will turn up the volume of my life and sing along as loudly as I can. I will be a role model for others to stretch beyond what they can see, instead of shrinking under the complacency of mediocrity.

PRAYER OF COURAGE

Lord, tonight I pray for the courage to be who You have called me to be. I want to be used as a vessel to do Your Will and I am passionate; but, at times my faith is challenged. I strive for my life to be an example to draw people to You, but sometimes I get tired of being different, tired of being criticized, and tired of being misunderstood. Today was a particularly rough day, Lord. I ask for a double portion of anointing to continue to walk in faith. Please revive my resilient nature, renew my strength, and overload my courage. I am honored that You have chosen me, and I thank You for the grace and favor You have on my life.
In You I Can Do All Things ... Amen

TODAY'S AFFIRMATION:
SURROUNDING SPIRITS

They say birds of a feather … As a person who strives to live an abundant life, I surround myself with other abundant thinkers. I do not give energy to people who are always starting something unproductive. This does not mean that I am anti-social or unkind, but I have the courage of my convictions. I protect my spirit to avoid other people's scarce mindset from infecting me. Including,

> People who always complain …
> People who discourage my dreams …
> People who criticize my faith walk …

I share my infectious, positive, and abundant spirit. However, I watch closely how my energy is impacted by others around me. Do I feel my best, encouraged, and supported when they are around me? Or, do I feel drained, craving space and wanting alone time when they are around? Am I the best version of myself when they are in my life? Or am I living at my lowest self? Based on these answers, I am bold enough to make the choice of who belongs in my innermost circle, whom I will trust, and whom I will engage in an intimate way.

TODAY'S AFFIRMATION: TRAVELING LIGHT

In my quest for an abundant life, I travel light. I do not collect experiences. I do not hoard pain. I do not hold bitterness. I do not get attached to a job. I do not endear myself to someone who does not value me.

In my most abundant life, I have learned to "let go to level up." I know that carrying too much baggage will overload the plane and inevitably I will crash and burn. So, I open the cargo door and kick out the pain of my abuse, disappointments, failures and rejections. I surrender all the baggage in the cargo hold that is dragging down my ability to soar. I do not remain loyal to a family that does not reciprocate that loyalty. This is baggage that I cannot hold.

Abundance means I have learned to graciously release people who are not good for me. I have to let go of that friendship that is distracting me from my best self. I have to let go of the fear of failure and jump off the cliff. I have to let go of the bitterness for those who have treated me wrong. I know that I cannot waste my life being bogged down in issues that do not belong to me. Since I am designed to fly high above the clouds, my wings cannot spread when I am holding too much.

TODAY'S AFFIRMATION: PLANTING SEEDS

I know that all abundance in my life is born of the seed God planted in me. That seed, if I cultivate, water, fertilize and nourish it, will make room for me and my family. It will also birth a harvest with plenty of overflow to give to others. I marvel at the beauty of a peach seed, watered, and nourished will grow into a healthy tree. That tree will then produce so much fruit that the overflow will feed the neighborhood. Then, the unused fruit will then drop back to the ground to fertilize the soil. That one seed provides a lifetime of abundance.

Once I understand this, I do not fret in my darkest days. I realize that seed inside me had to experience some dark environments underground. That was the season when my seed splits and grows. I also know that eventually, my seed will root, and the tree will break the ground into a beautiful plant. Therefore, I rejoice even in dark days; it just means I am being cultivated and prepared for growth. I also know that a season of overflow is on the way. I appreciate the seasons of my growth, and I do not spend them moaning about the darkness. Today may seem like I cannot see the way; but, I know when I break through and the sunshine hits my face, my overflow is in motion.

MY PROVOKING THOUGHT FOR THE DAY

A man's gift maketh room for him, and bringeth him before great men.
-Proverbs 18:16

Organizational and personal power is important and sometimes necessary to make change. However, there is no greater power than the ability to influence. The 5-Cs of influence include:

1) Competence - knowing and executing your
gift to the best of your ability.
2) Confidence - knowing what you have to offer and
being willing to learn what you have to gain.
3) Character - always acting in integrity.
4) Class - being gracious.
5) Courage - speaking truth to power.

TODAY'S AFFIRMATION: RELEASING CLOSURE

I do not need closure. Closure is a great trick of the enemy that will keep me distracted from the abundant life God promised me. I do not know why my mother gave me up for adoption, but she probably does not either. I stay future focused on the path God is taking me, and I choose not to hold open a wound that I can never heal. I do not know why my wife cheated on me, but I will not obsess on whether it was someone better or what I did wrong. I accept that it happened, and I can learn and grow from it so that we can make it work. Or, I choose to move on from the relationship. I will not beg my boss to explain why I keep getting passed over for promotion. I will either accept it, get what I can from the experience I am gaining, and move on to a better opportunity. I will not continue to stay mad at the hit and run driver who took my friend away. I can find peace and joy in knowing that she is not in pain, and she is in community with Christ. There are things that will happen in life that I may never understand, but I refuse to live my life in the past. My continued growth is not conditioned on understanding why people do what they do. I know this is a distraction that I will not allow to consume me. My gifted time on Earth is too precious.

TODAY'S AFFIRMATION: PREPARING FOR SOLUTIONS

One of the most powerful things I practice in my abundant life is prayer. I meditate and commune with God daily, on every aspect of my life. However, I am not a hypocrite. I know that I cannot pray to God to solve a problem that I am not willing to resolve. I cannot pray to God for deliverance in a marriage that I am not ready to leave. I cannot pray to God to release the stress of a job that I am not willing to sacrifice. I cannot pray to God to fix someone else, when I am not willing to work on myself. Part of the commitment to my prayer life is to ask God for those things I desire, but I have to then believe that He will deliver them. Once I believe, I then prepare for deliverance. This means my mind and spirit has to be ready to receive the deliverance, and I have to be obedient to the instructions to come. If God chooses to deliver me by having me quit the job, I cannot then moan about the solution; I have to be ready to move. If God chooses to deliver me by having a lifelong friend walk away from our relationship, I have to be ready to experience my life without this person. I cannot refuse the solution because I do not like the package it is wrapped in. God, I stand ready today to receive solutions, instead of sitting in sorrow.

IT IS SOMETHING IN THE WAY THEY MOVE

How do you identify another abundant soul?

It is in the way they speak with optimism and joy;

It is in the way they show resilience despite problems;

It is in the way they encourage those around them;

It is in the way they refuse to sweat the small stuff;

It is in the way they dream big and believe in self;

It is in the way they give and receive love effortlessly;

It is in the way they connect and care about the world;

It is in the way they always seem to make it work;

It is in the way they look for the beauty in the world;

It is in the way they refuse to give up or be defeated;

It is in the way they move.

TODAY'S AFFIRMATION: REBUKING ENVY

In my abundant life, I am not jealous of anything or anyone. What God has for me is for me; therefore, I do not believe I have to engage in negative feelings and emotions. I recognize that jealousy is born out of a lack of confidence; however, I do not lack because God has already provided everything I need.

I do not bemoan my coworker's new promotion, even if it is the job I wanted. I realize that just means God has something better for me.

I do not act in a jealous way in my relationships; because I know my worth, even if my partner does not.

I do not begrudge my family member experiencing a positive life change, as I know to celebrate others' abundance as a gift.

I celebrate the miracle that is my life, and I find joy in what God has done in someone else's life as well. I do not waste precious energy coveting someone else's gifts and blessings, because I know there are plenty of gifts and blessings for me.

TODAY'S AFFIRMATION: FAITHFUL LIVING

I live in faith and not fear. I do not reduce faith to an emotional feeling. It is not a tingling in my spine, or an overwhelming instinct to shout. Faith is not a feeling. Faith is an action I take based on the unwavering belief that God has already provided for my good. I do not walk around telling everybody who will listen that I am a man of faith; however, I do not have any evidence of faithful living. As soon as something goes wrong at my job, I panic, afraid to lose the job; that is not faithful living. When I get bad news about my health, I do not fall apart; that is not faithful living. When I experience conflict in my marriage, I do not fall into despair; that is not faithful living. Faithful living requires me to act based on the belief that God is always working in my life and in my circumstances. I know that one of the best ways to demonstrate my faith is through my thoughts, words, and actions; even when things do not go my way. Who needs faith when everything is going great? Faith is most pertinent when I cannot see my way. Staying positive, taking the next step, and giving my all again tomorrow are evidence that I believe God is working this for my good.

TODAY'S AFFIRMATION: RETHINKING FORGIVENESS

I have heard many times that forgiveness is for me, and is not for the offender. However, what if forgiveness is not mine to give? I believe that one of the most abundant gifts I have been blessed with is grace and mercy. I do not have to hold the sins of the past done to me, because I know they are already forgiven. I believe that when Christ died for my sins, He also paid for the sins done to me. Therefore, what my father did is his own sin; it is not mine to forgive. How my spouse treated me is her own sin; it is not mine to forgive. How my classmate bullied me is his own sin; it is not mine to absolve. Since I believe that God will work all things for my good, I stay focused on the learning and blessing that God created from the circumstance; and, not the circumstance itself. I do not spend my life figuring out how to forgive others, or how to get closure for what they did to me. I simply live at the highest denominator of my life, and thank God for all my experiences. I am thankful even for those that caused me pain or harm. I grew stronger from it; therefore, I count it all joy!

TODAY'S AFFIRMATION: MAKING A FRESH START

A fresh start is within my control. I realize that a fresh start is not about my circumstance, but about my mentality. I can make a fresh start by changing my perspective about the situation, even in its midst. A fresh start is not a new place; it is a new mindset. Therefore, I do not have to be stuck in my hometown because I do not have the money to move. I can choose to level up my thinking right where I am. A fresh start may not be leaving the relationship, but it may be a new perspective on the value I bring to that relationship. I am not defined by my partner, and am not less of a valuable human if they do not validate or affirm me. A fresh start may not be quitting this job, but it may be a refusal to let a boss or coworker irk me and taking back my power. No one has power over me that I do not give them. Sometimes, I must work with difficult people; however, they cannot steal my joy. I will not be locked into a prison of my own making, and in my own mind. I have the power to change the things I value, the things I choose to give energy, and the way I feel about myself.

LOVE REDEFINED

Today, I redefine the love of my life from a new abundant perspective:

From a person who spends time with me to
A person who invests in me

From the way I feel about a person to
The way that person makes me feel about myself

From a person who is at their best to
A person who brings out the best in me

From a person who I pour into constantly to
A person who pours back with reciprocity

From a person who has a lot of energy to
A person who energizes me

From a person who I believe in to
A person who encourages me to believe in myself

From a person who is smart and accomplished to
A person who shares knowledge and wisdom

From a person who is aspirational to
A person who is inspirational

From a person who has all the answers to
A person who asks great questions

From a person who can do a lot for me to
A person who does a lot for everyone else

From a person who is beautiful on the outside to
A person who finds beauty in the world and in others

From a person who collects fruit to
A person who plants seeds

From a person who laughs at my jokes to
A person who spreads joy

From a person who tolerates my calling to
A person who pushes me toward my calling

From a person who completes me to
A person who is fully whole themselves

Love redefined.

TODAY'S AFFIRMATION: PLUGGING BROKEN BUCKETS

Broken buckets cannot overflow! No matter how much money or success I obtain, I will never have abundant freedom until I fix my leaky bucket. My bucket is the sum of the experiences in my life. I have had some very difficult ones, including the loss of my loved ones, failure, the lack of courage to follow by dreams, abuse in a past relationship, and a difficult relationship with my mother. However, I recognize that if I am unhealed from these negative past experiences, my bucket has a hole in it. God may send me blessings; however, I can never hold and overflow them to others, if my bucket is leaking. I cannot appreciate the new relationship God sent me, because I am holding onto the bucket hole of hurt from the last one. I am blocking the blessing of the promotion God has for me, because I am still bitter about being passed over for a job two years ago. I cannot be a good father to my son, because my father was not around and I lacked good role models. These are bucket holes. If I do not plug them up, I can never experience the overflow God intended for me.

TODAY'S AFFIRMATION: PERPETUATING ABUNDANCE

I recognize that God intended for life to be lived more abundantly. I also recognize that we have created a world that is based on the "have and have nots." We structure all our interactions on the ability to categorize people into groups by race, class, sex, or any other category that suits our needs for superiority.

Superiority is not an abundant thinker's concept. As a believer in Christ, I do not subjugate to anyone as below me, or capitulate to anyone as above me.

I do not pit one oppressed group of individuals against the other, for the sake of perpetuating a scarce mindset. When I hear someone say that we should be taking care of veterans before refugees, I know this is a false concept. God created abundant resources to take care of both. When I hear someone arguing on whether we should allocate money for education or food insecurity, I know this is a false comparison. There are abundant resources to provide both. I am an intelligent thinker and an abundant giver to the world. My job is to help the least of these, not prioritize them.

MY PROVOKING THOUGHT OF THE DAY

Are my prayers for …

Peace

Joy

Power

Abundance

Deliverance

Patience

Prosperity

moot?

Why do I keep asking God for gifts He has already given me?

TODAY'S AFFIRMATION: CONTROLLING MY MOODS

I am abundant; therefore, I am kind and not moody. Abundance breeds consistency. I have joy when I wake up in the morning, and I am not moved or swayed by every little inconvenience in life. When you interact with me on Monday morning, you get the same smile and kind disposition as you do on Thursday night. I cannot represent abundance and the love of Christ when I am mean-spirited, cold, distant, unhelpful, or selfish. I cannot change my mood every time something does not go my way, because I can control myself and my moods. I choose to have joy and be happy, because I can decree my state of being. I help people that I do not have to, and I do not expect anything in return. I share information, access, and knowledge with others. I share, not because I am required to, but because I chose to. I derive pleasure from making others smile, and I do not engage in manipulative or intimidating behavior with anyone. My spirit is big enough, and I am confident enough in my own contribution, that I do not need to shrink anyone else to increase myself. I am kind and consistent today and every day.

TODAY'S AFFIRMATION: TAKING BACK MY POWER

I take my power back. Today, I snatch back all the power I have given you all these years of my life. Today, you will no longer humiliate or criticize me for any of the number of things you invent to make me feel less than the powerful human being I am. I take my power back.

Today, you will never put your hands on me again, or even flinch as if you are going to. Today, you are not going to rise up to me in anger or disgust to treat me the way you feel about yourself. I am not the object of your hatred, you are! And, I no longer receive your negative and destructive vibes. I take my power back.

Today, I no longer beg for your attention, your affection, your time, and your respect. Your energy is no longer important to me. I refuse to offer you my amazing and positive energy, just to receive your negativity and distastefulness in return. I take my power back.

I have decided that companionship, particularly your companionship, is not worth the hit to my self-esteem. I will no longer hold the stress of trying to keep you happy at my own expense. Today, I take my power back!

TODAY'S AFFIRMATION: REJECTING FEAR

No decision made in fear will ever prosper. I know that my prayer to God for an abundant life will never become a reality, if I do not believe that God's grace made me worthy. It does not matter the blessing that God sends my way, if I cannot see, receive, or appreciate them. Fear is a blocker! Everyday God sends me signals of love and loyalty, and I must rid my heart and spirit of the fear. The fear blocks the flow of love, joy, and gifts from God.

He can always see and hear me, but I cannot see and hear him when blinded by the fear of rejection, the fear of failure, and the fear of being talked about.

I desire the prosperity God promised me, and God will always deliver. I will not choke off that prosperity, due to my inability to receive it in faith and full readiness of my birthright.

TODAY'S AFFIRMATION:
AFFIRMING SELF-TALK

I know that my words have energy, and I am so powerful that I can speak things into existence in my life. As I am fully aware of my power, I do not engage in negative self-talk. I do not talk myself out of the opportunities and blessings that God is preparing me for. I do not rationalize away the positive events, and I do not accept negative events into my spirit.

I do not denigrate myself, even in jest. I do not engage in self-deprecating comments, even in humor. I know that repeatedly diminishing myself will become a habit. I also know that continually depreciating myself also gives others permission to do so.

With my powerful words, I encourage and affirm my contribution, my gifts and my worth. I speak joy and prosperity into my own life, and into the life of those I touch. I use my words to encourage and support my family, my friends, my colleagues. I am in tune with the energy of others, and I offer the power of my words to enhance their lives.

MY PROVOKING THOUGHT OF THE DAY

Is life happening to me?

Or,

is life happening for me?

Perspective is everything!

TODAY'S AFFIRMATION: BUILDING MY STRENGTHS

As an awesome individual attempting to live my best life, I do not get hung up on my shortcomings. I know there is no such things as perfection; therefore, I do not expend all of my energy on just developing my weaknesses.

I have decided to spend just as much time figuring out what I do right, then I work on honing to make it excellent. I focus on strengthening those gifts that I already do well, and then maximizing them. This grants me the ability to live in positivity and affirmation. If I am great at organizing, I maximize it; instead of forcing myself to be more of an abstract thinker. If I am a great public speaker, I focus on perfecting that skill; I do not torture myself to be detailed oriented. I partner with someone great at the details and we shine together. I do not beat myself up, or feel shame for things I cannot do well. I affirm those things I can!

TODAY'S AFFIRMATION: PRIORITIZING WORK

As an abundant employee, I have an impeccable work ethic. I do this because I am an abundant human, and I offer my best to everything in which I engage. However, I do not allow any job to push me away from other things in life that matter. This does not mean I lack ambition, or that I do not care about optimizing my career. However, I recognize that my job is a means to an end, and is not the end itself. I am thankful that my job permits me a standard of living to take care of my family, and to derive satisfaction for meaningful work. However, I do not expect my job to show me loyalty. I understand that jobs are a business. There are seasons that my job will be a blessing, and seasons that may create stress. I do not get so attached to any job that I become slave to it. I do not permit it to create anxiety and health issues. I do not get so attached to any job that I am neglecting my family and friends. I keep it in its proper place, relying on the Provider for my needs.

TODAY'S AFFIRMATION: BEING RESILIENT

I know that I can do all things through Christ Jesus who strengthens me. This means that I am powerful and because of Christ in my life, I can win. However, it also means that I can work through the losses. An abundant life is not without challenges and tribulations; but, I can work through, work around, or move them out of the way.

I can survive this grief; I can make it through these tough financial times until my season of prosperity returns; I can deal with this health issue; and I have the stamina to care for my father through this bout of sickness. I can do this because I am strengthened in great times of dexterity, and I can handle bad times of incapacity. I have difficult days, but every day God chooses to wake me, I get up and do it again. I know that life works in seasons, and this season too shall pass. Until it does, I can do this! I have an abundance of strength, and an abundance of resilience, and an abundance of peace. I trust what God has put inside me, and I will summon the strength and courage to do His will daily.

TODAY'S AFFIRMATION: CHANGING PERSPECTIVES

As I transition to an abundant thinker, I have to change some of the old methodologies that have held me in bondage. I change my perspective on experience. All "experience is experience." All experiences offer me a lesson that makes me stronger, more resilient, more capable, and that enable me to grow. Therefore, I am grateful for every experience I have. I no longer separate experiences into the way they make me feel. I do not distinguish between negative and positive experiences. I know the only difference between a negative and positive experience is the emotion I felt that accompanied the experience. Therefore, I have negated the concept of failure. This is a drastic change from the way I used to think; so, it will take some time to get used to. Now, I am grateful for the relationship that did not work as much as I am grateful for the one that did. I learned both who I wanted to be, and who I wanted to be with. I am as grateful for the job I was laid off from, as I am for the job I ended up with. Both taught me not to be loyal to a company, but to be loyal to God's calling on my life. I am as grateful for the time with the loved one I lost, and the ones I still have. Both taught me to love hard today and to appreciate those who honor and love me. The experience is the lesson!

MY PROVOKING THOUGHT OF THE DAY

Three thoughts killers that guarantee scarcity, lack of success and joy … I eliminate those today.

Negativity - "that I am not good enough, will never achieve, am not worthy, cannot thrive." I rebuke these thoughts today … I am who God says I am. I am grateful for what God has done and live expectedly in the abundant life He promised me.

Rumination - I cannot forget the negative experience I had at 18, the rejection I suffered in my last relationship, the abuse I suffered as a kid … I rebuke these thoughts today … My past does not define me; I can turn my pain into power, and I am a survivor and not a victim.

Conflict - "Everyone is out to get me, I can't get ahead, it is a conspiracy, that won't let me succeed." I rebuke these thoughts today … God has promised me abundance and prosperity, and I believe that no weapon formed against me shall prosper.

PRAYER OF DELIVERANCE

Father God, I come before You tonight, needing help and deliverance.
I have made some choices that have not turned out the way I expected.
I know that even when I make bad decisions, You will work out
situations for my good. Therefore, I trust and need You to pull me out
this thing that I cannot pull out for myself. I ask for Your forgiveness
and redemption, Lord, so that I can quickly get back on track of doing
Your Will. Thank You for carrying my burdens, and releasing me from
having to drag this current mess I have made into my future. Thank
You, Lord, for everything You have already done for me and being here
to deliver me, yet again. With all reverence, love and respect, Amen!

TODAY'S AFFIRMATION: MAXIMIZING MY TIME

There are 1440 minutes in today. I have the same 1440 minutes today, as does the richest person or the poorest person in the world. I have the same 1440 minutes, as does a prince and a pauper. I have the same 1440 minutes, as does a CEO or a janitor. My background, education, circumstances, living situation and upbringing may not be the same as everyone else; but, the one thing we all share is the same 1440 minutes a day. And every day that God sees fit to wake me, I get to decide how I use those 1440 minutes. I will use about 600 of them to maintain my physical health, because my physical health drives my overall health. That leaves 840 minutes for my spiritual and mental health, to nourish and support my family and friends, and to leave a mark on the world. I can use those minutes to expand my mind and capabilities, to help someone in need, to challenge myself to excellence, and to stretch into something amazing. However, I will not burn through my precious life minutes gossiping about others, criticizing or maligning myself or others, binge watching TV, feeling sorry for myself, or obsessing about things in the past. When the clock strikes midnight, my 1440 minutes reset. Every minute I gave away to negativity, I never get back.

TODAY'S AFFIRMATION: SPEAKING LIFE

I am a powerful force and I have the ability to create the life circumstances I desire. I do not whine about my life, or beg about things I want; I speak them into existence. I decree the desires God has placed on my heart, and I know that I have the power to create them. I can envision, believe, mediate, and speak them into existence. My ability to create is unparalleled; so, I use my power responsibly and do not speaking negativity into someone else's life. My power works in integrity and in alignment with God's will for my life.

I desire joy, so I speak it.
I desire resources to help others, so I speak it.
I desire to get more education, so I speak it.
I desire a healthy body, so I speak it.

When I speak it, God dispatches Angels to move the energy of the earth to bend to my desires. I am this powerful, loved and favored; and, I know it. Opportunities open for me; God crosses my path with the right doctor; and God has a friend affirm me. I do not believe these are inconsequential. I believe that God is intentionally working them for my good, and I prepare my heart and life to receive.

TODAY'S AFFIRMATION: MAKING DECISIONS

As I live my most abundant life, I do not accept that life just happens to me. Of course, God is in control; but, I also know that God has given me a full range of choices that allow me to fully engage in my own life. Therefore, to be in the club of abundance, I make decisions. I say no; I say yes; but, I just say something. I am not complacent, sitting on life's decisions, waiting for them to work themselves out. I pray to God for deliverance, and then I stand up, speak up, motivate myself and others. I say no to the job that looks perfect for me, because it does not feel right. I say yes to the opportunity of a lifetime, even if I have to move out of the country. I say hell no to the man who checks all of the requirements on my "must have" list, but makes me feel small and unwanted. I say something. I do not watch my life happening, and then wonder what went wrong. I am accountable for my decisions, and understand that I may make choices that have negative consequences. I do not anticipate every life choice I make will be perfect; otherwise, I would not learn and grow into the strong and wise human I am meant to be. So, I do not procrastinate or regret. I am in tune with my spiritual instincts, and make the best decisions I can through prayer, reflection, and God's guidance.

MY PROVOKING THOUGHT OF THE DAY

If you're always trying to be normal, you will
never know how amazing you can be.
-Maya Angelou

Regardless of my favorite basketball team, I marvel at how awesome the great shooters are. I wonder what would happen if I modeled my profession after their game? First, their work ethic seems impeccable; big shots are not lucky, they are practiced! How much time do I invest in my craft. Even when I am good, am I shooting for great? Second, they seem to have a short memory. They miss more shots than they make, but they do not linger on the miss. They get back on defense, and come back to shoot it again. Am I still holding negative energy about that promotion I did not get three years ago? Instead, I will get back, retool, and take another shot! Finally, the best of the game show gratitude; not just celebrating the score or the win, but being gracious for the opportunity to play. If I modeled these attributes, just maybe, I could also be an MVP!!!

TODAY'S AFFIRMATION: APPRECIATING BEAUTY

I listen to beautiful music. An abundant mindset requires a real appreciation for the beautiful things in life. I certainly recognize the tragedy of the human experience. I also believe that when God made the earth, He said that it was "good." I appreciate how beautiful it is on a warm sunny day. I love the majesty that is a little toddler learning to walk. I love art and the canvas that is nature. I love the miracle that a tiny seed can grow to a harvest. And cheesecake ... who would have thought something so beautiful and sweet could come from cheese! And, I love music. God created beauty in this world to remind us of His wonderous nature, and to soothe us in hard times. To me, that gets no better than music that soothes my soul, makes me dance or cry, and moves my emotions in a way that other experiences cannot. Some of my most endearing memories are set to the soundtrack of my life. The ability to sit alone on a moonlight night, drinking a bottle of whatever I enjoy, and listening to jazz is what abundant living is all about.

TODAY'S AFFIRMATION: RECOGNIZING MY WORTH

I know that as an abundant thinker, I am enough! I enjoy fellowship and friendship as much as anyone else; but, I do not bank my joy and happiness on others.

My abundance means that I have more than enough inside me,
available to me,
and given to me,
to have joy every day.

Everyone that God places in my life as friends, family, coworkers, or partners were added, once I chose to seek God first. I value those God has gifted me, but I do not allow them to distract me from the joy and prosperity God has destined for me. As I live abundantly, others cannot steal my joy. Others cannot impact my ability to see myself as God sees me. Abundant thinkers do not need validation by others. I believe that I am uniquely and wondrously made by God, which is sufficient for me to live my best life.

TODAY'S AFFIRMATION: DOING MORE

As a person who strives to live an abundant life, I look for opportunities to do more than what is expected of me. I do not live at the minimum of my contribution; but, I strive to live at the maximum of my capabilities. I know that sometimes I will do more, and I will not receive an immediate return. However, to live an abundant life requires me to build an abundant way of thinking. Doing more becomes a way of life.

I volunteer for the project that no one else at work wants to do.
I am willing to take on more responsibility in
the family, when no one else can.
I will raise my contribution in my relationship during
this season, because my spouse cannot.
I will raise my hand to be the parent coach for my son's soccer team.

I do this because I believe in being involved in my own contribution. The more I engage, the more engaged my life feels. I manage myself to avoid becoming overwhelmed; but, I have abundant energy, time, and resources. I can overflow to those who are in my life and in my community.

TODAY'S AFFIRMATION: CONTINUAL LEARNING

I know that abundant thinkers value intelligence and seek daily growth. I may not be in a position today to get another degree, or to be involved with a high-profile project at work. However, one of the small ways that I grow my mindset is by learning a new word daily (even better is when that new word is in a different language). Expanding my language capability lets me communicate and express myself in a more elaborate and sophisticated way. The confidence I gain by having access to an abundance of words stretches me to a new level of maturity. It enables me to expand my diverse connections in the world. I am impressed with myself when I use antithetical, or tempestuous, or unequivocally, diminutive and benevolent in a sentence (and use it correctly). When I push my mind to maximize its capability, the larger it grows. I am not close to the full use of the intelligence God endowed me; but, I am not afraid of learning new things and expanding my mind, my circle, and my reach. I know that intelligence is not just about academics, but it includes the maturity to fully participate as a citizen on Earth. With a strong language and an increased ability to dialogue, I can use my communication as a strength to influence a wider network.

MY PROVOKING THOUGHT OF THE DAY

What if I took a chance on the vision God planted in me?

What if I just took one step in faith today to …

Call that publisher

Redo my resume

Fill out that mortgage application

Text her a "good morning"

Open that vacation savings account

Research how much student financial aid I could get

Register my business name

What if I just took one step in faith tomorrow?

TODAY'S AFFIRMATION: EMBRACING CHANGE

I can change my mind. Growth requires change, movement, side steps, and redirection. Sometimes it means that I can outgrow my environment, my circumstances, my relationships, and my ideology. As an abundant resident on the planet, I know it is a natural part of maturity into the abundant being I was meant to be. Who I love at sixteen may not be who I love at sixty-one. That is not a lack of loyalty; it is a recognition that I may grow into a more abundant relationship. My career ambitions at twenty-four is nowhere close to what I am doing at forty-two. That is not a waste of time; it shaped the understanding of my experiences and exposed me to the next thing in my life. I do not live in the town where I was raised. That is not about a lack of appreciation of my upbringing; it is just a reflection that I was on a path to other experiences. I do not beat myself up for changing my mind. The more experiences I have, the greater I stretch my mind, my opportunities, and my strengths. I have my own path. As a gracious and abundant thinker, I do not judge others' path, and I do not regret my own. I am a collector of abundant and rich life experiences. I do not let others dictate my path; abundance comes in thirty-one flavors!

TODAY'S AFFIRMATION: NO SHRINKING

Abundance in my mind and spirit mean that I have the ability to positively influence others in the world. Therefore, I do not shrink or hide my beautiful spark of life behind others; nor do I let them dim my light. I do not associate with others who cannot handle my awesomeness, or resent my beauty. I do not diminish myself to another's insecurity by relenting who I was meant to be. I recognize that letting my light shine in the world is not about how outgoing or personable I may be. A light shining in darkness can be a big smile and boisterous laugh, or it can be a quiet confidence and sweet spirit. However, I do not hide my light to avoid being seen. I do not sit behind my spouse and let her dim my shine; we shine together. I respect and honor my boss's position, but I do not shrink behind him in the meeting. I speak up when I have something appropriate to offer. I do not forgo the opportunity to offer the wisdom and strength God has gifted me. I realize that meekness is a fruit of the Spirit; but, it does not mean I am invisible. Meekness recognizes that all the capability comes from what God offers me.

TODAY'S AFFIRMATION:
LIVING CURIOUSLY

I am an abundant thinker with a big brain. I am intellectually curious. I know that an abundance of intelligence is not about how many answers I have; but, it is how many great questions I ask. I push my brain to its maximum capacity, by seeking to understand things that interest me. I am engaged in the things around me and love learning. I want to know how things work; I want to explore why I think and dream the way I do. I want to understand the impact I can make in the world. I do not fear what I do not know; I just view it as an opportunity to grow. I do not carry insecurity when I am around someone I view as more intelligent than me. I believe God is exposing me to someone who can help me expand my mind, thinking, and opportunities in the world. I surround myself with high level thinkers who can help me level up, and I use the moments to grow myself. I am also willing to take the time to answer questions from someone who thought enough of me to pick my brain. I know that by sharing knowledge, I get even more in return; so, I am abundant with my giving.

MY PROVOKING THOUGHT OF THE DAY

What if you were never mine to lose?

What if you were on loan for a season to teach me …

How to be a giver
How to have compassion
How to experience love
How to think big
What pure joy feels like
What having peace feels like
What being encouraged feels like
What being supported feels like
About kindness
About graciousness
About successfulness
About truthfulness

What if I dared to honor you instead of grieving you?
What good could I do in your name?

TODAY'S AFFIRMATION: IMAGINING THE BEST

As a person who strives to live an abundant life, I am not oblivious to the realities of life's journey. Circumstances can be difficult. People will do me wrong; however, I do not let the difficulties of life jade my perspective. I cannot experience joy, if my first reaction to everything I do not understand is to fill in the holes with the worst-case scenario. Even if I am unsure of someone's intentions toward me, I seek to understand first. I do not accuse; I ask. I do not think everyone is out to cheat me, because my last friend did. I do not assume that every boss is a jerk, like the last one was. I do not presume that I will be rejected, just because I was last time. I realize that this may leave me somewhat vulnerable. Being open to possibilities of positivity does not make me weak; it reinforces my power. Just because I choose to be an open-minded person, does not mean that I make poor choices and expose myself to danger. I have enough discernment as I continue to watch and pray, that I will recognize when a person is taking advantage of me. I trust that God will always protect me in every circumstance. But, to live life at its maximum, I must learn to trust in God's intention and His will for my life.

TODAY'S AFFIRMATION: MAKING IT PLAIN

I know that when God gifts me with a vision, I am to write it down and make it plain. As an abundant energy, I use vision boards to document and visualize the dreams and visions that God has placed on my heart. I may not know exactly how they will all be accomplished; but, I am obedient to the impulse that visualizing, and writing gives them life. I know that I cannot just have unrealized visions in my head for my entire life. The first step to actualizing those dreams is for me to acknowledge them, and then to write them down. I then read them daily, and I pray to God for revelation. I know that as I give my visions this energy, God will then reveal the next step in the vision's materialization. I do not minimize or criticize my own visions. I also do not rationalize why they can never come true. I believe in the desires God has placed in my heart, and I fully adopt them. I am careful of who I share the visions with; I do not expose those visions to friends, family or anyone who may try to kill or diminish them. God placed them on my heart for a reason, and I keep it as a beautiful secret between us, until He makes those dreams come true.

TODAY'S AFFIRMATION: NO REGRETS

I have lived an abundant life that I am proud of. I have made plenty of mistakes and had plenty of joys; but, I have not lived a life of regret. As I abundantly age, I am considering my legacy, and what I want to leave for the next generation. I can leave an abundance of financial resources for my kids. However, I am also focused on leaving an inheritance of integrity, character, excellence, and love. I want to be known as the person who left it all on the table; a person who lived a life of faith and not fear; and a person who challenged myself and grew every day. I want my legacy to be one of refusing to settle in love, in happiness, and in growth. I will have a life well lived that was messy and non-linear. I will have a life that was full of intimacy and joy. I will have a life that God promised me. I will shred the nonsense of my past mistakes, past hurt, and past disappointments. My legacy will not be of shame and hurt; but, I will walk with the sun on my face. When God decides on my last day, I want the first memory of me to evoke a hearty laugh. I enjoyed my life, and I reminded everyone else of the beauty and faith that is this human experience.

TODAY'S AFFIRMATION: THINKING POSITIVITY

I have an abundant imagination. Therefore, I think in terms of possibilities, and not limitations. I know that I cannot embrace change and cannot grow if I focus only on what I have to lose. Overly thinking about loss enforces a mindset of scarcity; but, recognizing what I have to gain by a moment, an opportunity, or a life change is what abundance is all about. If I believe my gain will come at someone else's expense, then I miss the point of abundance. I enjoy my blessings and share them, knowing that more are already on the way. I do not compete in life with anything or anyone, other than my former self. I know that whatever dreams God plants in me are available to me; so, I open myself wide to His Will and prepare to receive as big as I can dream or think. I may not know anyone in my family who has traveled around the world; but, why not me? If God has planted it, I am packing my bags. If dreams of being a lawyer has been planted in my spirit, I am not worried about how I am going to pay for law school; I start studying for the test. I allow myself to go with the dream as a sign of how big my life can be.

BECAUSE I CHOOSE TO …

I look at the world around me today and I see …

Mass School shootings
The climate destruction of the earth
Racism, Sexism, and other isms that promote inferiority
Homelessness
An overwhelming number of children without food
Trauma and Tragedy
Abuse and Destruction
… a lack of morality and integrity

I look around my life today and I see …

My spouse and I are not on the same accord
My desire for a new promotion declined
My want for a new house deferred
My physical body is ailing
My job is providing me stress
… a lack of accomplishment and authority

How can I possibly experience joy when this is my life?
How can I spread happiness and make a difference?

Because … I choose to.

TODAY'S AFFIRMATION: PUSHING MY GROWTH

I know that growth requires sacrifice. It also requires being pushed to the brink. Even though I exercise regularly, muscles grow when pushed to the point of failure. Muscles failure can cause the muscles to stimulate, which can lead them to grow bigger and stronger. I know that this is the way life works, not just with muscles, but with everything else. Tribulations may come my way, and it may push me to the brink of failure. However, my spirit and mind are already programmed to heal themselves, if I let them. In that process, I grow bigger and stronger. Therefore,

losing my loved one is muscle failure that makes me stronger;
a difficult boss is muscle failure that makes me more resilient;
a health scare is muscle failure which makes me more diligent;
having lived in poverty is muscle failure which makes me gracious.

I am working out today and everyday. Watch me grow!

TODAY'S AFFIRMATION: BEING ENOUGH

I am worthy and I am enough. I am not the worst of my mistakes. I am not the lowest common denominator of my life. I am not the pain and disappointments of my past.

I am worthy and I am enough. Every day, I choose to see myself the way God sees me. I am made in His image.

I am worthy and I am enough. I have been granted grace, which has filled in the gaps of my failures and shortcomings. Since God does not hold them against me, neither will I. I no longer care how others will judge me. I will learn to let go of my past; so, that I can grow into what God has for me.

I am worthy and I am enough. I do not need to prove myself to anyone else. I am not competing with anyone, except the past version of myself. I do not engage in negative self-talk, and I do not self-destruct my own potential. I do not shift shape for the convenience or pleasure of others; and I do not give energy to those who do not see my worth. I am worthy and I am enough.

TODAY'S AFFIRMATION: JUMPING THE TRAIN

Good morning to a new day! I wake fully engaged into my life, and into my contribution today. I am confident and focused on God's plan for my life. I am a train of awesome! Now, I welcome others to jump on this train; but, I will not slow down or allow myself to be sidetracked, due to pettiness and insecurities. It is my intention to give my full attention to the abundance of life today. I am eating my favorite sushi for lunch today; I am calling the person who makes me smile; I am going to read a book I have been wanting to. I am going to enjoy every meeting I go to today; even if it is a useless meeting, with no agenda and no purpose. I realize it for what it is, and I will not let it frustrate me. I am who I am supposed to be, and my light shines bright. Not to generate attention for my own glory, but to honor the gifts that God has given me. I have gratitude every day; but, today I am on an overload of thankfulness. Everything in life is not perfect, but who said it was supposed to be? With this knowledge and affirmation, I am off to start my day!

SETTING THE STAGE

I set the stage for how I am treated ...

I can't expect others to believe in me when I do not believe in myself.

I can't expect others to be faithful to me when I am unfaithful to myself.

I can't expect others to be truthful to me when
I am not truthful with myself.

I can't expect others to invest in me when I refuse to invest in myself.

I can't expect others to value my uniqueness when I do not value myself.

I can't expect others to see my worth when I do not see it myself.

Today, I affirm that I am bold, strong, confident, and
graceful. I am authentic to my beliefs, and I invest in my
dreams and desires with my own resources and energy.

TODAY'S AFFIRMATION:
UNDERSTANDING THE GOOD

As an abundant believer, I know that God works everything for my good and His glory. However, everything for my good is not necessarily for my pleasure. Sometimes I had to make my daughter eat green vegetables, even though she did not like the taste. I understood that green vegetables were good for her, to build her immunity, and to provide the necessary vitamins and minerals for her healthy growth. Maybe losing my job did not feel good, but it opened the opportunity for God to bless me with a business. Losing my marriage was difficult and stressful; however, it taught me the real value of me. Being diagnosed with a chronic condition was scary, but, was the impetus to teaching me to value and respect my body and health. Grieving my father was difficult; but caused me to question the legacy I want to leave for my kids. I know that God keeps His promises; but, an abundant life is not necessarily one free of challenges. Abundance means that God uses every experience, good and bad, or challenge lost or won, to work together for my good. So, even in my darkest days, I cannot lose.

TODAY'S AFFIRMATION: COMMUNICATING MATURELY

As a sophisticated and mature member of the abundance club, I know how to communicate. I own the responsibility to communicate my thoughts, wants, values, needs, shortcomings and desires. I do not expect others to interpret something that I refuse to communicate. I value what I have to say; therefore, I say it in wisdom and with purpose. If I need, I ask. If I want, I express. If I desire, I articulate. I do not diminish the power of my words and my thoughts for the sake of others' feelings, or others inability to communicate themselves. One of the most precious gifts endowed to me by God is my voice, and I use it for His glory. I do not permit anyone to tell me to "shut up and sit down" because what I think, and how I feel matter. I do not waste my valuable communications on those who refuse to consider what I have to say. I have a high self-worth. While I do not choose to comment on everything, I expect my input to be taken seriously and contemplated in a respectful way. I remove myself from any situation in which my ideas and my words are viewed as less than others. What God has for me is for me, including my voice!

PRAYER OF POWER

Father God ... thank You for making me so powerful, strong, and granting me the ability to do all things in Your name. You have blessed me that I do not have to live in victimhood, or live distressed, or live oppressed. You have given me the power of my entire mind. Help me to unlock all the wisdom and potential You have given me. Push and challenge me to grow beyond what I can see, and what You have built me to be. Provide me opportunities and access to impact the world toward Your Will. I can handle it Lord; use me. Amen

TODAY'S AFFIRMATION: NO COMPLAINING

Today, I walk through the day, and I refuse to complain about anything. As a full card-carrying member of the abundance society, I do not complain. I realize that if I practice complaining, it will become a habit; then it will become a way of life. I refuse to mirror this destructive behavior of others. They complain about the rain, but the sun is too hot. They complain when they get promoted, and complain when they do not. They complain when they are hungry, and complain when they are too full. They complain when they are married, and they complain when single.

I do not send complaining vibes into the atmosphere. The more I complain, the more I look for something to complain about. Instead, I strive to speak with gratitude about everything today. If the traffic is heavy, I am grateful for the alone time to think. If my boss adds a new project at the last minute, I am grateful that I have the capability to complete it. If it is pouring rain, I look forward to the flowers tomorrow. I realize that when I practice gratitude, I begin to look for something to be grateful for.

TODAY'S AFFIRMATION: HAVING A BAD DAY

I am having a bad day. I am tired and a bit overwhelmed; but, I need to wash these clothes. I forgot to pay my credit card bill, so the credit card company dropped my credit limit … off one late payment! My father needs my help this weekend to file his taxes, and I am not sure how I am going to manage that between the kids' activities and having to work. The toilet upstairs still needs repair; so, I have shut it off for now and have the kids to use the guest bathroom. My car registration expired yesterday. I am having a bad day!

Ok, now that I have gotten that out, bad days exist! And a bad day is not a bad life. Everything that is inconvenient does not require a negative reaction. I will wash the clothes tonight while I sleep. Forget that credit card company; I was planning to go debt free. My father will come over this weekend to watch the kids while I work overtime. I have another toilet, and I can take the car in next week. I am having a bad day; but, a bad day is not a bad life. I stay calm, plan, and do what I can when I can. I do not stress over things so small …

TODAY'S AFFIRMATION: MAINTAINING CONTROL

As an abundant contributor to my own life, I focus on the things that I can control. I do not live frustrated, or concerned with what others think. I can control my own voice, my own decisions, and my own choices. I may not be able to control what happens to me; but, I control how I choose to respond and feel about it. I may not be able to control whether others receive what I have to offer; but, I control my intentions and my effort. My input belongs to me, and the output belongs to God.

I do not judge or try to control others. I do not need to talk others into what they should do. I do not need to convince others to agree with my choices and decisions. While I value advice from those who love me, my choices belong to me, and I am fully accountable to them. I control my moods, and they do not control me. I control my happiness, and I do not condition it on others' view of me. I control my body and my mind, and I strive to live the way God intended for me.

I AM POWERFUL AND I KNOW IT!

I celebrate my awakening and affirm my worth, my joy and my contribution. I decide to live a great day with intention.I remind myself of my potential and my possibilities. I do not have "never" in my vocabulary. I tap into all the power already planted in me to overcome and thrive.

I speak kindness and prosperity into those I encounter today, even if they do not speak it to me. Since I have an abundance of joy, I can share it with someone who cannot seem to find their way. I shine brightly today; so, brightly that no can dim my glow.

I rebuke negative thoughts, negative emotions, negative self-talk, and negative energy. I do not accept limitations today, and I release all the mental barriers keeping me from excellence. I can do this because I am powerful, and I know it.

TODAY'S AFFIRMATION: SWEATING THE SMALL STUFF

As an individual who strives to live an abundant lifestyle, I do not sweat the small stuff or create unnecessary stress. I will not waste my energy today on useless matters that do not matter. That I was cut off in traffic is beneath the frequency I vibrate on; we both got to the light at the same time. That a passenger cut in line to get on the plane does not irritate my spirit; we both got to the same city at the same time. That someone else was assigned the project I wanted at work does not crush me; what God has for me is for me. That I did not pass my college entry exam the first time is of no consequence; the person who passed the first time and when I passed the third time got us the same degree. I do not engage in competition with others for the sake of competing. It may inconvenience me; however, I control my mind and my emotions. I save my previous and high value energy for matters that propel me toward God's purpose for my life. I engage to care for my family, whom God has provided for my responsibility. I engage to demonstrate excellence and humanity in my giving and living. I mind only those things that matter.

TODAY'S AFFIRMATION: MAXIMIZING MY GIFT

I realize that I can only experience an abundant life, if I am fully maximizing my gift. I know my gift because it is the thing I know how to do that I do not know why I know how to do it. It is something that is just planted in me and comes naturally. I can ignore my gift, fail to develop it, or take it for granted; however, I cannot get rid of it. It came as a seed planted inside me at birth. This is why it is called a gift. Therefore, I choose to take the time to discover it, nurture it, and to use it for God's glory. It is okay that my gift may not be as obvious as others' gifts may be. Some people are gifted at sports or singing or other activities that lend themselves to be visible. That is fine; however, a gift is not a gift because it made me famous. My gift may be something much more subtle. For example, I may be great at planning and organizing things. I may have a knack for mechanics, and the aptitude to understand machinery. I may have a gift of inspiring and motivating others to discover their own gifts. Regardless, I foster my relationship with Christ, and I learn to listen to the Holy Spirit guiding me to discovery. Once I embrace my gift, I can build it and learn to maximize it for the betterment of others.

IT AIN'T WHERE YOU'RE FROM; ITS WHERE YOU'RE AT

I may be from an impoverished area, but poverty is a state of mind.

I may be from a broken home, but brokenness
is an emotional state of being.

I may be from a small rural town, but small-
minded thinking is a state of consciousness.

I may be from an abusive environment, but
powerlessness is a mental state of condition.

The only state that matters is the state of my own mind.

I only live a small life when I have a small mind; and,
a big abundant life comes from big thinking.

Our thoughts are the engine that drives our actions,
and releases the power for it to materialize.

TODAY'S AFFIRMATION: LOOSENING RESTRAINTS

When God formed me, He intentionally made me uniquely and wondrously; therefore, I am not constrained by the limits of environment. No matter that I am from a small country town; I am not ashamed of it, and I am not restrained by it. No matter that I am from the housing projects; I am not ashamed of my environment, and I am not contained by it. No matter that I grew up in a house where I had the best of everything; I am not ashamed of my privilege, and I am not defined by it.

Where I am from is just the start of my path and does not define my outcome. I use everything I have been exposed to as part of what I have to offer to world. I embrace and honor my experiences, but I do not allow them to control the choices I make. Just because my father was an alcoholic, does not mean I am predestined to follow in his footsteps. Just because my friends did not graduate from college, does not set the upper limit for what I can achieve. Just because I do not know a surgeon, does not mean I ignore my calling and passion to be one. My starting point was just a start.

TODAY'S AFFIRMATION: DEALING IN ISOLATION

I am in a season of loneliness. How can I experience abundance when I feel so alone? There are a few people around me; but, it seems that for no reason at all, people are turning away from me. I do not feel the same alignment with my friends, my spouse, my loved ones as before. My tolerance in my relationships is frayed. And every day it appears that I am becoming more and more isolated. I realize that God works all things for my good; therefore, I may not like this feeling, but I look for the blessing in this experience. I acknowledge that there are times when God will allow my surroundings to clear out, and for my life to run empty. However, I also know that during these times, God will refill the void with blessings that I do not have room enough to receive. God will make space in my head and my heart; therefore, I can dream big and contemplate the visions He planted. My season of loneliness creates a pathway to greater righteousness, and it creates the ability for God to fully use me for His glory. I have heard it said that separation comes before elevation; therefore, I embrace this today in full anticipation of the elevation to come.

MY PROVOKING THOUGHT OF THE DAY

What would I choose to do in my life, if I was guaranteed not to fail?

What would I choose to do in my life, if I refused to fail?

What would I choose to do in my life, if I removed
the concept of failure from my mind?

What if failure did not exist?

TODAY'S AFFIRMATION: LIVING IN EXPECTATION

In my quest to live my most abundant life, I live expectedly. I believe in God's promise; so, I expect to be graced with the desires of my heart. I am excited about my life and what is to come. I anticipate new opportunities each day and expect possibilities. I do not waste my life engaging in unworthy talk. Such as, "it doesn't matter, I will never get it anyway." Or, "why try, they will never let me succeed." Even when something does not appear to go my way, I do not lose the expectation of something better. I know that challenges are part of the journey; so, I expect them as well. I am strong and resilient enough to withstand and overcome them. Life's challenges do not break me down, or make me lose anticipation of the great things. I know He plans to prosper, and not to harm me. Therefore, I am on the lookout for prosperity. A life challenge, while it can be daunting and may cause inconvenience or emotional pain, ultimately cannot break me. It feels good to wake up every day knowing that prosperity waits for me. I do not surrender these expectations, regardless of what I see. I know my faith walk is by belief, and not by sight.

TODAY'S AFFIRMATION:
STRIVING FOR EXCELLENCE

I do not strive for perfection. I recognize perfection as a trap of unhappiness. Perfection is unattainable. This is not because I lack magnificence; but it is because of how perfection is measured. Perfection is an objective measure determined by a society of imperfect people; therefore, it has no significant meaning. Who determined that I got a perfect grade? An imperfect teacher. Who determined that I did a perfect job at work? An imperfect boss. Who determined that I am a perfect husband? An imperfect wife. Perfection is not the goal.

Instead, I embrace excellence. Excellence is a subjective measure based on my maximum capability. Only I can determine if my efforts are excellent. I measure excellence by giving ny best effort at work, whether or not my boss recognizes. I measure excellence by maximizing my talents to help someone in need, whether or not others value it. I measure excellence is letting my works, energy and attitude be of glory to God. I measure excellence by living at the top of my life today. This enables me to be a shining example of God working through my life, and by drawing others to Christ!

TODAY'S AFFIRMATION: PURSUING CHRIST

Today, I am not focused on obtaining another material thing. I know that my quest for abundance is not about the pursuit of more things; but, the pursuit of a more intimate relationship with Christ. I seek God first, and then all things will be added to me. As I open myself wide as possible for God to use me, abundance then comes to me; I do not have to chase it.

God will unlock opportunities to stretch beyond what I can see. I am abundantly vulnerable, I am abundantly available, and I am abundantly giving of myself. I am confident that my heart's desire is already prepared, and I will not miss out on them by chasing after the wrong things, people or goals. I have access to everything my Father has predestined for me, and I will stay obedient and open to receiving them.

TODAY'S AFFIRMATION: SHOWING GRATITUDE

I recognize that an abundant spirit is marked by gratitude. I am grateful for my health, family, job, relationships, and other important things. As I grow in grace and relationship with Christ, I learn to maximize the power, wisdom, and abundance that He has already given me. I spend time learning and meditating on my gifts to learn how to use them to contribute to the world. I am fully confident in the dominion over all things God has already gifted me. God has gifted me as an authorized user on His credit card. I can charge my ambitions, my health, my life, my possessions, my family, my job, and my joy to this card without needing extra permission. I know that He has already eliminated my spending limit, and has already paid the bill. Therefore, I walk through my faithful life unencumbered with the stress and worry of how I will be provided for. I trust the Provider, and I believe that when I insert that chip into the card reader, the transaction will go through. It is my birthright, and I am confident enough to claim it.

THE FORMULAS FOR ABUNDANCE

Give and it will be given to you.

Ask and you shall receive.

Knock and the door shall be open to you.

I am trying this today!

TODAY'S AFFIRMATION: GAINING FROM GIVING

I am amazed by this simple life principle that my gain comes from giving. Scarcity, lack, and poverty come from withholding unduly. I look around my life today and rejoice that my gains in wisdom come from sharing knowledge and opportunities with others. I believe that my financial prosperity is based on giving to help others. When I give freely of my love, love comes back to me abundantly. Therefore, I do not withhold it because I have been hurt or wronged in the past. Whatever desires God has placed on my heart today, I will practice giving it away, and expectedly wait for God to multiply it. I give without the expectation of reciprocity from others; because, loyalty to others is misplaced. I expect all good and perfect gifts to come from God. He will reward and provide abundantly all that I could ever receive or ask. Today, I shift my mindset to giving and believing that God's word is true!

TODAY'S AFFIRMATION: MOVING AND GROWING

An abundant life requires growth and movement.

I cannot be the same person I was ten years
ago and have an abundant life.

I cannot think the same way I did six years ago and live an abundant life.

I cannot have the same circle of friends representing
the old me and expect abundance.

The old me represented my level of maturity at the time. I know that abundance requires taking chances, taking steps forward, and making life moves. I do not sit back and wait for life to happen to me. I walk boldly into new avenues; even if those moves present new challenges. If I do not take a step, I will look up years later and be in the same place. I recognize that sometimes what appears to be a step back is a set up for a level up; so, I do not live in regret. I give myself permission to change my mind, to move to another station in life, and to follow the dreams planted in my heart.

MY PROVOKING THOUGHT OF THE DAY

Because God built me to grow, the provisions
He has given me are always temporary.

I have to be willing to release a provision that has outlived its usefulness.

I have to be willing to let go of my current
season for a new season to begin.

Temporary blessings do not stop being blessings
because we have outgrown them.

Refusing to change and grow will keep me from
the next level God is elevating me to.

TODAY'S AFFIRMATION: PRACTICING POSITIVITY

This morning I wake with a positive, can-do spirit. The most powerful gift I have been given is the ability to control my life. I can never achieve abundance with a negative mind. I practice positive living by expressing gratitude for what I have already been given. I practice positive living by looking for and expecting the good to occur in my life. I practice positive living by smiling and spreading joy to others.

This does not mean that I do not see or ignore negative events. It simply means I choose to view my life perspective through a positive lens. I realize the power of my whole mind, and I have the ability to reshape and reframe a situation, circumstance, or event to receive the positive from the experience. I also know that this takes practice, discipline, and energy. It is easy to criticize, to find negativity, and to complain about things we experience. But, if I exercise this positivity, I will begin to train my mind and my heart to see life through a positive lens. Then, positive thinking becomes my way of life.

TODAY'S AFFIRMATION: REVALUING TITLES

As a flourishing member of the abundance society, I do not put a lot of stock in titles. I may carry many titles, Mr., Husband, Mrs., Wife, Dr., Supervisor, Director, Vice President, Owner, Mother, Father, Friend, Influencer, Socialite and more. However, I am sophisticated enough to realize that titles do not make me worthy. I live by the principle that I reap what I sow, so I focus on sowing the seeds of the return I want. I cannot achieve abundance of respect, loyalty, graciousness, influence, power, or honor by demanding it from others using my title. This is fleeting and not sustainable.

If I want loyalty as a husband, I give it to my wife. If I want respect as a supervisor, I give it to my employees. If I want honor as a father, I give it to my children. Real power is only achieved in abundance by giving and sharing real power; it is not by the superficial power the title implies. My rewards are endowed by the Creator; therefore, any recognition by others is just icing on the cake.

MY PROVOKING THOUGHT OF THE DAY

If I am reaping stress, maybe I am planting seeds of discontentment.

If I am reaping insecurity, maybe I am planting seeds of doubt.

If I am reaping mistrust, maybe I am planting seeds of dishonesty.

If I am reaping scarcity, maybe I am planting seeds of a hoarder.

If I am reaping wisdom, I must be planting seeds of knowledge.

If I am reaping financial abundance, I must
be planting seeds of investment.

If I am reaping good health, I must be planting seeds of healthy living.

If I am reaping joy, I must be planting seeds of happiness.

TODAY'S AFFIRMATION: CHOOSING HAPPINESS

I am happy today! I know this because I have chosen to be happy today. There are multiple things that I can allow to bring me down today. For example, my job sucks and so does my coworker; my spouse is nagging me agin because he is discontent in the relationship; my car did not start this morning; and my kids are on my last nerves running around and missed the bus.

Despite this, I am happy today! I am in a good mood, because I control my mood. I could surrender to life's irritations and inconveniences today. I could react to those things that cause me pain or stress, but I do not have to. I am stronger than my negative circumstances. I can also choose to remove myself from people, places, situations, and events that negatively impact me most. I win every day that I choose to. This does not mean that hard times will not touch me; but, I am steadfast that no weapon formed against me will prosper. Because of that, I have no need to walk in shame, hate, defeat, or negative energy today. I am up and at 'em, and when I am in this mood, I am dangerous (in a good way!)

TODAY'S AFFIRMATION: SPEAKING LIFE

Today, I watch what I speak. I realize how powerful my mind and thoughts can be; therefore, I am focused on dedicating my energy on things that support my abundant life. I am open to talking about ideas and the more I engage in this dialogue, the more ideas God will feed me. I am open to talking about how to love and give more. The more I dialogue about this, the more love and joy I will receive. As an abundant recipient of life, I do not waste time talking about other people. I do not have time for such a useless exercise of my energy. I contemplate how I can use my gift more. I research how I can be more productive. I engage in ways to maximize my contribution to my job and family. I do not waste time talking about how my friend's wife cheated on him, how my cousin got arrested, how my friend's bad kids got suspended from school, and how my son's friend did not get into college. I am glad to offer myself as a sounding board for those I love, but I do not gossip for the sake of gossiping. I know this is an unproductive exercise that wastes my precious time and energy. I stay focused on what I can offer today.

PRAYER OF LOVE

Lord, You are the love of my life …

Thank You for being madly in love with me …

I am madly in love with You …

Amen

TODAY'S AFFIRMATION: REFLECTING ME

What I see in others exists in me. When I see fear in others, it reflects my own lack of confidence. When I see beauty in others, it is because I see beauty in me. When I see defeat and misery in others, I am mirroring a negative view of myself. When I see potential and possibility in others, it is because I see the potential and possibility in myself. When I criticize others' life and effort, it is because I lack the confidence in my own. When I see vision and promise in others, it is because I believe in the promise and vision in me. When I dwell on the hate and prejudice of others, it is because I have allowed those feelings to infect me. When I am attracted to the petty gossip of others, it is because I am distracted from my own goodness. When I am encouraged and lifted by the spirit of others, it is because like souls recognize each other. When I judge others' decisions and actions, it is because I feel less than myself. I know that what I see in others reflects me; therefore, I look for the greatness in others around me. I look for the positivity and faith in others, which affirms my own. I look for the enduring and resilient spirit, which encourages me on my journey.

TODAY'S AFFIRMATION: HOPING FOR FAITH

I decree abundance into my life, instead of just hoping for it. Are hope and faith the same thing? Now faith is being sure of what we hope for, and being certain of what we do not see. Faithless hope is not productive, since faith is the engine that activates the hope. I hope I will get accepted to college, because my GPA is not high. I hope that I will get selected for this new job, because I only have six years' experience. I hope he likes me and will call back, since the first date was lukewarm.

Hope is based on a perspective that I do not deserve something, which helpless feeling. I am an abundant person; therefore, I walk in faith and have the power to decree those things that I hope for. If God places a new job on my heart, it is already mine. If God has placed a new relationship into my spirit, he will call again, or someone else (better) will. If God has shown me the opportunity to go to college, I will get accepted to this college or another one that is better for my situation. I declare and decree it, by the power given to me through Christ. I do not just hope for things, I am able to generate them through thinking and speaking them into existence through faith.

MY PROVOKING THOUGHT OF THE DAY

I have the power …

To prophesy and speak life into myself and others

For my body to heal itself

To change my mind

To remove myself from unhealthy situations

To make choices that benefit my life

To be an intercessor for my children's lives

To be happy

For my soul to be in peace

To elevate …

TODAY'S AFFIRMATION: ANTICIPATING GREATNESS

I wake today in anticipation of big things! I am destined for an abundant existence; therefore, I believe it and carry myself in this promise today. I think, speak and act as big as I have been ordained to be. I reject small thinking, small minds, and small acquaintances today. Small thinking breeds me to fear, motivates me to covet, and causes me to complain. Big thinking enables me to faith, to grace and to gratitude. I have all the evidence I need of how big my life is supposed to be based on the Holy promise:

I will be made exceedingly abundant, more abundantly than I can think, or ask, until my cup overflows, and that I may prosper in all that I do. I will be made abundantly prosperous, and have every good and perfect work from above, as my blessings will be poured down until there is no more room to receive. I am promised riches and honor in life, as well as abundant peace and abounding hope.

I dream big, think big, speak big, act big, and make big decisions; and, I have nothing to fear as God is true to His promises!

TODAY'S AFFIRMATION: TRUSTING THE PROCESS

I know that if I want an abundant life, I have to trust the process. Every natural example around me tells me that abundance and overflow come after a growth process. This growth process usually requires some discomfort and pain; however, out of this process reveals the blessing.

I cannot experience the abundance of fruit from the apple tree until it has completed the process. The seed has been buried; then it has lived in darkness; then it has expanded to crack open; then it has rooted; then comes the breakthrough to form a beautiful and prosperous tree.

The most beautiful relationship in my life is with my child. I only experienced after months of pain, discomfort, sleeplessness, and heartburn. After this season of darkness, my child expanded and rooted, then came the breakthrough of deliverance.

Spiritual growth works the same way; therefore, I do not fret during the darkness as my breakthrough is on the way.

TODAY'S AFFIRMATION: SHOWING GRATITUDE

As an abundant thinker, I am growth-oriented and growth-minded. I am always seeking ways to mature emotionally and spiritually. Therefore, I understand that I will undergo multiple changes in my life. I do not bemoan these changes; I welcome and participate in them. Changes in jobs, relationships, locations, and status are inevitable. Sometimes I will be initiating the changes, because I may need new surroundings. Sometimes the changes will be prompted, because God need to reposition me to serve a purpose. Regardless of the reason, change does not throw me into a tizzy. I know that when God asks me to put something down, it is because He wants me to pick up something greater. I believe that all things work to the good of those who believe; therefore, I trust that when it is time to let go of one thing, I rejoice because better is coming. I did not want to get laid off, but I will use the opportunity to start my business. I did not want my relationship to end, but I take the opportunity to go back to school. Change is healthy and builds resilience. I do not shy away from it, and I do not complain about it. I count it all joy.

YOU MISSED IT

You had me, but …

you pulled away on the verge of my breakthrough

you refused to believe in me on the cusp of my destiny

you were not willing to invest in me on my precipice of awesomeness

you criticized me on the path to self-discovery

you recoiled against me on the evolution to the vision

… and you missed it!

TODAY'S AFFIRMATION: PROTECTING MY ENVIRONMENT

Abundance is influenced by my mind and my environment, both of which I control! I do not have the capacity to develop beyond what I believe. I also do not have the capability to grow beyond my environment. Therefore, I have create and protect an environment that supports my abundant thoughts and lifestyle. This means I cannot spend all my time with unproductive friends. My environment will dictate that I will have to settle my thinking to fit my friends' mindset, or I will have to isolate myself to preserve my thoughts. I cannot spend significant amounts of time in a relationship with someone who does not believe in themselves. The way they see themselves can cause me to dilute or diminish myself, or force me to remove myself to avoid being a relationship with a lack of parity. I cannot flourish at a job that diminishes me or requires me to behave in an unethical way. Regardless of how strong willed I may be, I am either going to jeopardize this position for my beliefs, or I will risk being compromised. When I recognize that I am in an environment that may be detrimental to my abundance, I began to pray and prepare for deliverance and change.

TIRED ...

I am tired of being sad
I am tired of being blue
I am tired of being ignored
I am tired of you ...

I am tired of feeling strange
I am tired of disrespect
I am tired of being sick
I am tired of neglect ...

I am tired of begging
I am tired of being weak
I am tired of explaining
I am tired of a future bleak ...

I am ready to be rewired
I am ready to be acquired
I am ready to be inspired
I am tired of being tired ...

TODAY'S AFFIRMATION: HAVING COURAGE

As an abundant thinker, I have courage. I do not shy away from life's opportunities, because of what I have been told should be my life's path. I want to dedicate my life to adopting children. Despite society's expectation that I am supposed to marry in my 20s, work a traditional 9-5 and retire at 65, this is not in my spirit. I walk in the courage of my convictions. I do not want to go to college and want to pursue my dream of being an artist. Despite society's expectation that I will make less overall money over my lifetime without a degree, I walk in the courage to follow the life I imagine. I do not want to follow in my father's footsteps to run the family business; I want to fix cars as my passion. Despite society's expectation that I should carry on the family legacy, I have the courage to follow my own dreams, and I put together a business plan for my auto repair shop. I do not want to stay in this marriage that has no passion, no joy, and does not light my fire. Despite society's expectation that I should stay married for a lifetime, I will pursue the love of my life. Only I am accountable for my choices. No regrets!

TODAY'S AFFIRMATION: VISUALIZING BEAUTY

Today, I choose to see beyond my reality, and I allow my vision to unfold beautifully and fully into my consciousness. My reality may not be the job that I want; but, I have a vision of something bigger and better that I embrace today. My current reality is not the financial freedom I desire; but, I have a vision of an abundance of financial wealth that I began to visualize. My current reality is an unhappy relationship; but, I have a vision of a warm, engaging, and prosperous union. I may not have the friends, exposure, family, or happiness I thought I would have today; but, I know that once God has placed it in my spirit, it is available to me. I allow these beautiful visions to come fully into view.

As I think on these visions, I began to speak on them; I began to speak them; I then write them down to make them plain; and I began to act on them. As a result, God meets me at the point of belief, and He delivers the desires of my heart into my new reality. Once I believe, my vision becomes real.

TODAY'S AFFIRMATION: SHOWING GRATITUDE

My circle of family and friends looks completely different from when I was young; from ten years ago, and from two years ago. I look around and my circle of family and friends is much smaller than it used to be. I look around and I am isolated to a few people that I choose to have close to me. These are not circumstances to regret. I am content that some people who cross my path are not meant to be in my circle for a lifetime. I am content that God will place some people in my life for just a season. I embrace this change, and I accept is as part of the growth process. There may be some people who grow with me who can stay in my circle. Others had a chance to grow with me; but, they were not ready for growth.

If they are not ready for the challenges and discomfort that comes with growth, I do not regret that I have outgrown them. The only real loyalty is the loyalty to God's calling on my life. This will involve moves, changes, and redirection over time. I will not stagnate my life waiting for someone else to embrace their abundance. You can rock with me, or I will rock alone! Change is inevitable.

ABUNDANT FAITH (ON THE DL TIP)

Faith does not come by going to church every week. Faith does not come by worshipping.

Faith does not come by helping the poor.
Faith does not come by doing.

Faith does not come by reading motivational books. Faith does not come by reading.

Faith does not come by being a good Mom or Dad.
Faith does not come by good works.

Faith does not come by morning meditation.
Faith does not come by silence.

Faith does not come by surving something difficult.
Faith does not come by seeing.

Faith only comes by hearing the Word of God, which facilitates belief and activates God's blessings in your life.

TODAY'S AFFIRMATION: DEFEATING DOUBT

No doubt! The biggest obstacle to my dreams and desires is doubt. I know that doubt has killed more dreams than failure ever will. Failure is not an emotion, and it has no more power than I allow. If I attempt something that does not work out, that is a one-time occurrence. It is nothing more. However, I was not destined for my dreams to come true on my first attempt. Maybe they will not come true on my second or third attempt. However, what kills the dream is not how many times I make the attempt. It is when I begin to doubt that any attempt will be successful. Belief is my biggest advocate, and doubt is my biggest obstacle. If I consider that failure is just a step in the process to teaching and preparing me for the inevitable success, then it is not failure at all. I take it at face value and use it for growth. With this perspective, failure is just a platform to get to the success. Doubt infects my thoughts, and it makes me give up before success can be achieved. The dream or vision is mine as soon as God plants it in my spirit. I do not doubt it, or I will never achieve it. I do not give up on it, because it is taking longer than I thought. I do not speak life into doubt; so, it does not fuel my actions.

TODAY'S AFFIRMATION: CONSTANTLY PRAYING

As a fervent consumer of life, I pray constantly. I pray every morning, every time I eat, and every night. I pray at picnics, during traffic, and on the way to work. I pray when happy, when sad, in sickness and in health. However, I know that prayer has two parts to the activity. Whatever I ask for in prayer, I must also believe that I have already received it. This is the formula. It is a two-part communication with God. I ask, meaning that I actively communicate with the Lord. I talk about the desires of my heart, and I listen to God impart His desires for me. Then, I must believe; NOT that God will do what I ask, but I believe that God has already done it. I am not waiting for God to do something for me; but, I am praying for revelation of what He has already done. I then need to get up in belief, and act on what I have already been blessed with. Now, when the mail is delivered to the mailbox, I need to go to the box to retrieve it.

TODAY'S AFFIRMATION: CARRYING POSITIVITY

I am on guard today, because I know that mindsets are contagious. I believe that if I carry a positive mindset, that power can infect those around me. I must be careful about consistently surrounding myself with those who have a negative mindset or disposition. A negative mindset is also contagious. People who do not believe in abundance, do not live in joy, do not have peace, or do not strive for the best in their life, can influence me to be content with settling for less. People who think small, criticize others, and live in doubt can influence my ability to think big, appreciate others, and walk in faith. A small thinking friend cannot understand or value a big thinking friend. I am wired for big things; therefore, I value the friends in my circle based on their mindset. I value a friend who lifts me, celebrates me, honors me, reciprocates my love, believes in me, and who reinforces the beauty and power inside me.

MY PROVOKING THOUGHT OF THE DAY

I control my own mind …

If I let you offend me, you can manipulate me.

If I let you define me, you set my boundaries.

If I let you judge me, you have my power.

If I let you criticize me, you distract my destiny.

But, only if I let you …

TODAY'S AFFIRMATION:
EMBRACING MORE

I know I was meant for more; I can feel it. I have always known that I was different. I do not think I am superior to anyone. But, I think differently about the world. I talk differently than others around me. I can tell that I should be doing something greater, but I am not sure of what that is. I just know this job is not enough. I know that living for the weekend is not enough. I know that binge watching TV, and occasional trips to the movies is not enough. I was made for something bigger than this. I am destined for an abundant life, but I cannot see my way to it. I believe that for me to experience the abundant life I want, I have to make some hard life choices. Maybe that means I have to change jobs, or relationships, or location, or mindset. I just know that where I am is not enough. This does not mean I am necessarily unhappy. Contentment and gratitude for what God has blessed me with is not mutually exclusive. However, I know that to live a life of abundance, it is time make some big choices. But, I am made for this!

TODAY'S AFFIRMATION: WALKING MY PATH

I am conscious of my path in life. Paths can be righteous, narrow, straight, upright or plural. I am grateful for my path, and I do not expect it to mirror everyone else's path. I recognize that since God made me uniquely, my path is also unique. There are times my path will be well lit, and other times it will be dark. My path will have roadblocks and detours; however, it is still my path. My path will have hills and valleys; but, it is still my path. Some seasons, my path will be in parallel with someone special, and sometimes my path will be isolated. Sometimes my path will split, and I will have to choose which way to go. My path is not diminished, because it included a valley of abuse. My path is not more distinguished, because it included a season of financial abundance. It is just my path, and I walk it boldly and in reverence to God, who walks before me to clear the way. There are rest stops along the way; but, they are not designed for me to live there. I stop to allow my soul and spirit to rest; however, life is about walking the path. I cannot stand still too long; otherwise, my path stops in its tracks. I believe to enjoy a healthy, long life, I have to keep walking.

TODAY'S AFFIRMATION: MANIFESTING MY VISIONS

I am in tune to the visions God has planted in my spirit. I understand that visions require belief, not sight. Sometimes God is working a vision in my life that takes time to manifest. My vision is a pact between me and God, and I do not worry that I cannot see how the vision will come to fruition. I do not own the output; but, I believe God is working on my behalf and creating a need, audience, or place for this vision that I may not be aware of today. Therefore, my focus is on my input. It is my job to believe in the vision God placed in me. It is my job to prepare my mind and heart and to make room to execute when God says "go." It is also my responsibility to manage those in my innermost circle of influence. Continually permitting people close to me, who do not believe or support me is a product of my own doubt. This will result in a dream deferred, delayed, or denied. This may mean seasons of isolation on my journey. I also am comforted that when I feel doubt or need affirmation, God will send someone to encourage my spirit. Today, I am focused on being immersed in the Spirit, and I am trusting God to do the rest.

MY PROVOKING THOUGHT OF THE DAY

I do not seek the perfect person I want ...

I seek first the Kingdom of God ...

And, trust God to send the person I never knew I needed.

TODAY'S AFFIRMATION: NO CHASING

I am uniquely and wonderfully made, and I dream big dreams in color. I do not chase people, success, or experiences. Chasing feels like desperation, and I am not desperate. What God has for me is for me; therefore, I do not have to beg or run after it. However, when I put myself in the best position, what I want finds me. If I want an elaborate career, I do not chase it; I become an elaborate thinker and the career finds me. If I want a successful relationship, I do not chase it; I exude the characteristics I want in a relationship, and it finds me. If I want open and transparent communications in my life, I give it. If I want loving intimacy in my marriage, I give it. If I want peace and joy in my family, I offer it. If I want more money, I maximize my value and I offer it to those who need it. In this way, money finds me. I focus on value, instead of funds, and the funds will follow. This is the way I show up, and the way I think about the world; therefore, it does not require any extra effort on my part.

TODAY'S AFFIRMATION: CONQUERING ENEMIES

I do not waste time on my enemies and their negative intentions. I know that God will bless me with overflow in front of my enemies. My enemies may have an intention to harm me; but, I know that no weapon they form against me can prosper. I know that my enemies have to watch my head being anointed with oil, and they have to watch my cup overflowing.

My overflow provides substance not only for me; but, for those who have encouraged and supported me; for those whom God has put in my path; for those who have invested in my dreams. When I overflow, I can impact everyone else in my circle. I can then lift them with me.

I do not need to worry about my enemies. I just trust God to move them out of my way.

TODAY'S AFFIRMATION: CHOOSING HAPPINESS

I am happy today; because, I choose to be. I finally understand that happiness is not an emotion or a feeling; but, it is a choice. It requires an intentional decision to exemplify gratitude and joy. When I know that it is a choice, it is impossible to be stolen from me. Of course, things will happen in life that make me sad or that drain my energy. I do not ignore these circumstances; but, I have just decided to have power over them. Even if this means that I need a little downtime to deal with those negative emotions, I can choose not to stay there. I allow myself to express them, be comforted in them, and then I adjust my disposition back to the spirit of happiness.

I do not have to conform to the feelings others expect me to have. I do not have to grieve the way others expect me to do. I do not have to deal with rejection the way others expect me to. I can choose to see the lesson and grace in the situation. I can choose to celebrate the life of my loved one, instead of mourning the loss. I can choose to use the rejection as a platform to launch into a better alternative. I choose happiness right now …

I AM SO IN LOVE ...

With your smile and with your heart

With your humility and with your humanity

With your graciousness and with your gratitude

With your investment and with your integrity

With your faith and with your fearlessness

With your courage and with your compassion

With your joy and with your generosity

With your peace and with your power

With your honor and with your grace

... With You

TODAY'S AFFIRMATION: HONORING A WEALTHY MINDSET

The love of money is the root of all evil; however, I know that I can have money and not love it. I also know there are many people who do not have money and love it enough to do anything to get it. I also reject that being broke and poor is a badge of honor. The honor is not in the money or lack thereof; it is in the mindset.

Poverty is not a condition; it is a way of thinking and acting.

Wealth is not a condition; it is a way of thinking and acting.

As I strive to make a better life for myself and my family, I know that money is a useful tool to take care of myself and others. It does not provide the security; God promises to provide for all our needs according to His riches in glory.

TODAY'S AFFIRMATION: REJECTING SCARCITY

Jesus fed thousands from five loaves and two fish. I am impressed by how God takes lack and converts it to prosperity. The disciples impressed upon Jesus that they did not have enough to feed the multitude of people who gathered. They viewed the situation from a perspective of scarcity. However, Jesus took the means and provided for the thousands, which then overflowed to leftovers. I rejoice that God does not just meet my needs; He overflows me. Therefore, I will live my life through the lens of abundance, and not of lack. I can only see a certain amount of money in my account; but, I know what God can do. I cannot see enough time in my life to go back to school; but, I know what God can do. I do not see anyone in my life who will help me through this situation; but, I know what God can do. I have been called to do something impossible and pull off this project at work with limited resources (five loaves) and even less time (two fish); but, I do not fret because I know what God can do.

PRAYER OF REVERANCE

Through the Holy Spirit, Lord I come before You humbly and in reverence as God You are. Thank You for using me, loving me, providing for me, and choosing me to represent You on this Earth. I will be obedient to Your Will for my life. I will humbly serve where You tell me to serve. I will respectfully go when and where You tell me to go. I will dedicate my life as a living sacrifice and in all things stive to give You the glory. You are God all by yourself and I honor You. Thank You for my life more abundantly. All Praises to the Father, the Son and the Holy Spirit. Amen

TODAY'S AFFIRMATION: SHOWING GRATITUDE

I have an abundant life. I declare it, and I believe it. I know that what I declare and believe becomes self-fulfilling. When I believe, I will look for and see opportunities in life that others cannot see. When I do not believe that abundance exists, I will only see obstacles and challenges.

I can see the mountain; but, I am confident in my way around, through it or I will move it. Mountains may present themselves, but I do not have to worry. The mountain has no power over me; therefore, I do not wait for opportunities. I am open to them through my lens of abundance. Where others see barriers and difficulties, I see a moment to grow. Where others see grief and pain, I see an opportunity to get stronger. Where others see chaos and conflict, I see a chance to bring calm and harmony. Where others see despair and gloom, I see redemption. I know that I see the world in a different way than most of the people; but, I am not discouraged. I have figured out how to live in prosperity.

TODAY'S AFFIRMATION:
MEETING MY NEEDS

I am excited today that God promised to meet all my needs according to His riches in glory. Well, since God is all powerful, that means His riches are unlimited. Today, I leave for work in joy and contentment, knowing that all my needs will be met. I rejoice in knowing that it does not matter what my needs are. My needs can be food and shelter; but, can be sanity and continued peace during chaos; it can also be strong lungs, despite my family history of lung disease. My needs may even be unknown to me; which means I do not have to articulate them to be met.

I am abundant beyond measure, and I do not have to carry the responsibility of understanding what my needs are. I can just trust that they will be met in Christ's name. I can enjoy my day and sleep tonight like a baby; knowing that my Father has already made the provisions for me.

PUTTING MONEY IN ITS PROPER PLACE

Money is not the root of all evil; it is the love of money that is the root of all evil. It is possible to love, but not have money. It is also possible to have, but not love money. Use these rules of having and enjoying the money, without the money having you. Money is …

a tool to provide, it is not the Provider.
not connected to my righteousness.
something I want to reap, so I am willing to sow in integrity to earn it.
something I return in abundant measure to
help those who are the least of these.
one of the things I use to spread good in the world.
great for my life, but something I will never let define or imprison me
an opportunity to practice good stewardship
in the gifts God blesses me with.
a means to help others, but not to be used
as a means of power over others.
impactful when I give it as opposed to spending it.
not the end, but a means to an end.
one of the many blessings God has provided for me that I am grateful for

NEGATIVITY NO-NOS

I rebuke negative thinking today, and I replace those thoughts with positive affirmations of prosperity and peace. To stop myself from thinking negative, I have to recognize it and catch myself immediately. I am thinking negative when I am …

Overwhelmed with thoughts of the past,
including abuse and hurt, loss and grief.

Unable to focus on today, and unable to see
simple solutions to simple issues.

Complaining constantly about things over which I
can change; but, lack the will or courage.

Irrationally worried and stressed about the future,
in a way that paralyzes my present.

Overly moody in my emotional state, and easily
frustrated by life's common circumstances.

I re-shift my perspective today … negativity defeated!

TODAY'S AFFIRMATION: SEEKING GOD FIRST

I am thankful today that God has made life so simple for me. All I have to do is to seek first the Kingdom of righteousness, and things will be added. Not a few things, not some things, not a spattering of things over the course of my lifetime; but, ALL things. This is the essence of abundance, and I know how to achieve it. Every day, I will strive to seek God's Will and my calling. This is achieved through a more intimate relationship with Him. He will reveal all things He has provided for me, and I simply need to remain ready to receive. I need to seek God first; not my kids, not my marriage, not my job, not my house. As a result of seeking God first, all those things will be added. I will keep God as the priority, believing that my relationship with Him is the foundation of all other things that He will provide. I am excited to know that my righteousness is guaranteed, and I do not have to hope for joy, love, peace, or prosperity. It has already been promised. I thank the Lord for being true to His promises.

I AM WHAT I WANT

I realize that reaping what I sow also applies to
the energy and attitude about my life.

If I am passionate and gracious, I receive passion and grace.
If I am contentious and doubtful, I receive negativity, and disbelief.
If I am full of praise, I receive mercy.
If I live my life expecting favor, I look for and receive favor on my life.
I choose to be loving and kind today, and I will
receive love and kindness in return.
I want promotion and advancement, so I promote and advance others.
I want peace, so I share a peaceful disposition
to others I interact with today.
I want joy, so I carry happiness and a joyous spirit in my heart today.

I cannot expect to receive what I am not willing to give. I give it in
abundance, knowing that it is promised to return in greater measure.

TODAY'S AFFIRMATION:
GIVING ABUNDANTLY

Abundance is not obtained; it is given. I desire to live an abundant life; therefore, I must give abundantly. I now understand that abundance does not come from holding or hoarding what I have been given; but, from my willingness to share those gifts with others. Today, I commit to give of myself, my knowledge, my time, and energy to help someone I do not have to.

I do not give with an expectation of return from those I give to. God has already promised that the retrun is a gift from Him. Even more exciting is that the measure I give, will be measured back to me. If I give an abundance of positive energy to those I interact with today, I will get it back in abundance. If I give someone else an opportunity to shine today, my opportunities will be limitless. If I share my expertise, I will grow in wisdom. Imagine living a life that I cannot lose.

TODAY'S AFFIRMATION: BURNING PASSIONATELY

I am a ball of fire! My abundance overflows, and it burns so hot that it warms everyone in my atmosphere. I cannot enjoy an abundant life if I am passive or indifferent about my life. My fire purifies those exposed to it; it lights the pathway for me and others; and it provides warmth when it is cold. My fire is contagious and can spark life, love, and change to those in my immediate circle. Imagine what my spark of fire can do if it spreads across the world! Why me?

Why not me? The most impactful people in the world were just regular people. They chose to make extraordinary choices, engage in meaningful things, and maximize their gifts. I commit to make myself, my household, my community, my neighborhood, my country, and my world a reflection of the good God created. As an abundant thinker, I care about more than just myself. I know that when I prosper, my prosperity provides an avenue for all those around me to also prosper.

MY PROVOKING THOUGHT OF THE DAY

Why do I keep asking for things so small from an Almighty God?

Do I not believe …

God can do it … this is a lack of salvation

God will do it … this is a lack of faith

God will do it for me … this is a lack of worth

Or, that I can handle it?

TODAY'S AFFIRMATION: IMMEASURABLY BIG

I am an abundant thinker; so, I think big. However, I rejoice that whatever I think or ask, God can do more than I can imagine. That means no matter how big I can think, dream, or imagine, God will do immeasureably more than that. That sounds like limitless possibilities to me. I will stop being afraid today of dreaming big, because this Word tells me that God will do it through His power that is at work within me. God's full measure of power works through me.

Today, I am going to show up with all power, walking in the confidence of God working through me. I am showing up in the spiritual arrogance that I can do all things through Christ Jesus, who strengthens me. I do not have to psych myself out about this; God promised it, and has already provided for it. The realization of this promise, is only conditioned on my measure of faith and preparation to receive it. God, bring it!

TODAY'S AFFIRMATION: ABUNDANT BLESSINGS

I am reminded that God promised to always bless us abundantly in all things. I celebrate the power of this in all things big and small, and always. There is not a time I am required to go without. I understand that God's blessing of abundance means that I do not have to live in scarcity of joy, health, money, opportunity, or peace.

In this one promise from God, I have the freedom to eliminate all fear of having to go without. This is the basis of my abundant attitude. I can take some life risks; I can follow my calling; I can step out on faith to do those things that I have been called to do. I know that God ordained them for me, and has already provided the way, means, and resources to achieve. Now that I am unlocked, there is no limit on my potential.

TODAY'S AFFIRMATION: EXERCISING DOMINION

In case I underestimate the enemy's purpose, it is not to inconvenience me, or to make me sad, or to make life harder for me. He comes to steal, kill, and destroy my family, my spirit, my life, my calling. I do not take this for granted. I count it all joy that the enemy only has the power I give him. Since I am made in God's image, I have access to all power God has granted me. I can exercise dominion over all things of the earth.

I do not fear the enemy, because God comes that I may have life more abundantly. I am not barely scraping by, living at the lowest denominator of my life; but I am the head, and not the tail. He endows me with abundance of everything, including eternal life and salvation. He endows me with the resources to supply my physical and mental needs, my emotional well-being, and my financial resources. I wear the entire armor of God every day and leave no holes of weakness for the enemy to be successful.

TODAY'S AFFIRMATION: BURNING PASSIONATELY

The enemy is going to send someone my way today who will try to talk me out of my dreams. Funny thing, the enemy is going to use someone I love and respect. I expect this, and I am not moved by it. I believe God will honor me, if I do not let anyone talk me out of the vision and dreams He has planted in my spirit. I will not permit anyone, even those I love dearly, to make me doubt my dreams.

I am going to write the vision God planted in my Sprit ten times on a piece of paper, and I am going to read it repeatedly all day. Whenever I feel doubt, I will take out this paper, renew this affirmation, and speak life into my vision. It will be a particularly tough day, but I know that bad days do not last. My destiny will not be defined by my worst day.

I have already forgiven my naysayer because they are not even aware they are allowing themselves to be used. But, I will not permit their doubt to generate mine.

MY PROVOKING THOUGHT OF THE DAY

If I am feeling negative today, I can change my thoughts to positive.

If I am feeling devalued and diminished, I can speak life into myself.

If I am feeling irritable and discontented, I can evoke joy on demand.

If I am feeling disconnected, I can reach out to seek connection.

If I am feeling powerless, I can generate power from the Source.

If I am feeling pain, I can turn that pain into power.

If I am feeling grief or loss, I can transform that grief into honor and recognition.

What I am feeling today is completely within my control!

TODAY'S AFFIRMATION: TRUSTING THE CONVICTION

I am feeling uneasy about something I know the Holy Spirit is convicting me to do. I do not feel as if I have the skills, talent, courage, or resources to achieve this big goal God has put in front of me. Although I acknowledge this feeling, I know God never asks me to do something He doesn't also equip me for.

Therefore, I will trust the conviction. I will take on this new responsibility, apply for this mortgage, write the first page of this book, and accept this job offer. I believe that what God ordained, He will ensure success.

I will commit to be diligent in my obedience to His calling. When it gets hard and I want to give up, I will take a breath, offer gratitude for the trust God has placed in me, and I will keep going. Even in times that I feel overwhelmed, I will rise to the challenge because God trusted me. For all that He has given me, I am prepared to return a measure of my devotion to His Will in my life. Starting today!

THE CHECKLIST FOR WEALTH

Am I financially wealthy? Financial wealth is not a predefined number. Financial wealth is not comparative to other people. Financial wealth is a state of consciousness on your individual relationship with money, and its use.

Use this checklist to test your financial wealth. Give yourself one point for each statement you think applies to you.

1. Wealthy people make moves in silence. You do not hear a wealthy person talking about how much money they make or have. It is crass and immature. It only serves to be comparative, and to establish superiority over those who have less.

2. Wealthy people do not seek money. Wealthy people focus on ideas, inventions and opportunities that return money. Money seeking is a small-thinker's activity. Wealthy people understand true return on investment comes from ideas that changes the world.

THE CHECKLIST FOR WEALTH

3. Wealthy people take care of their mind, body, spirit, and wallet. Wealthy people know that it is illogical to be out of balance and expect sustainability. Wealthy people know that being deficient in any part of your life makes you deficient in every part of your life.

4. Wealthy people have gratitude for what they have been blessed with, and they have a healthy perspective. Wealthy people do not live in worry or stress about money, and they understand there is a stream of it always available if you have ideas.

5. Wealthy people are not obsessed with designer possessions. Wealthy people focus on building wealth for generations to come in their own families, as opposed to building wealth for the designer's family. Wealthy people are not defined by the brands of others.

6. Wealthy people give willingly to help others. Wealthy people believe that money is a tool that can be used to change the condition of the world. They do not hoard money for themselves, they share it for the good of mankind.

THE CHECKLIST FOR WEALTH

7. Wealthy people make a difference. It does not matter how money they can acquire, if it is sitting in the bank, it is of no use to anyone else.

8. Wealthy people do not care about keeping up with anyone else. Wealthy people celebrate what others have been blessed with, and they are not comparative. Wealthy people are not insecure, and they do not need to prove their wealth to anyone else.

9. Wealthy people do not panic. Life is not a zero-sum game. Wealthy people do not care if someone else gets their slice of the pie. Wealthy people own the bakery and just make more pie.

10. While everyone else invests in stocks, bonds and mutual funds, wealthy people invest in ideas, talent, and opportunities. Wealthy people understand that sustainable financial wealth has a source, and that source is people.

THE CHECKLIST FOR WEALTH

11. Wealthy people do not waste days or time living in the past, being sour over missed opportunities or relationships. Wealthy people do not plot revenge or other useless mind exercises. Wealthy people live in the present and move on to the next idea.

12. Wealthy people do not need or lack because they are not needy or deficient.

13. Wealthy people enjoy their life and keep a healthy perspective that money plays in their existence.

14. Wealthy people seek purpose. They realize that when you connect with your purpose in life, your purpose will make room for you and generate plenty of financial resources. They also know that purpose gives for a lifetime, not just a moment in time.

THE CHECKLIST FOR WEALTH

15. Wealthy people are diversified, and thry have multiple interests and diverse experiences in life. Wealthy people have an intellectual and emotional curiosity about the world, that enables them to see and embrace opportunities.

16. Wealthy people do not embrace fear. They understand that an extraordinary life will require extraordinary choices, decisions, and changes. They are willing to live a higher existence, which will include some risk and uncomfortable growth.

My Wealth Score:

14-16 – you got it!
10-14 – you may be rich in spirit, but keep going
Less than 10 – be inspired!

TODAY'S AFFIRMATION: MAKING BOLD CHOICES

I know that to live abundantly, I must make bold choices today. I am not going to stay limited by my circumstances, my environment, or my surroundings. Regardless of what I cannot see, I have faith to take big swings in life. The power of my gifted mind has unlimited capacity. Regardless of my limited resources, I am going to stretch beyond what I can see. I may not know the right steps to reach my goals; but, I am going to step anyway. I know that all things work to the good of those who love God, and those who keep His promises. I do not fear failure, because I trust that God will never leave or forsake me.

Mediocrity is not in my nature. I am built for excellence and have the capacity to change the world. That journey starts today, with one step toward my destiny. I can do all things through Christ Jesus, who strengthens me. I refuse to live in regret; I am going to take a chance on the love of my life; I am going back to school for the degree I always wanted; I am going to adopt the child I never thought I could have. Bold choices yield bold results!

TODAY'S AFFIRMATION: REBUKING NEGATIVE THOUGHTS

I own my thoughts. God planted a seed of growth and prosperity in me, and I know the enemy wants to plant weeds to choke out that seed. I rebuke the enemy's ability to infect my thoughts today. I have access to all power, I am worthy of His promises, and I receive His grace and mercy with gratitude and thanksgiving. I reject attempts from anyone who tries to make me feel and live small, to feel unworthy, and to believe thoughts that diminish me. I will not feed my mind or body negative energy, negative food, or negative thoughts today. I know that joy is a fruit of the Spirit that cannot be robbed from me, even in the darkest and most difficult of times.

With this renewed confidence, I approach this day with an expectation of abundance of health, wealth, joy, and peace. My boss, not my family, nor my friends can take that away, because it is not theirs to take. However, I share these abundant gifts freely with all those I meet today, because my supply is unlimited.

TODAY'S AFFIRMATION: ELIMINATING SCARCITY

I do not believe in scarcity. There is ample water, food, money, natural resources, education, health, and opportunities in the world. Although these resources are provided to all of us by God, we have distributed them in an uneven way. Therefore, some people have lots, and others have none. I am aware of this; therefore, my abundant tendencies drive me to share what I have been given with those who have need. That principle does not just apply to the richest one percent of people; but, to everyone who has all they need and has overflow. And, that includes me. This does not mean I always have money to give. I have my health, my time, my resources, my knowledge, and my positive spirit that I can share. I realize I may not get this back directly from the person I gave it to; but, that is not the reason I give. I give of my time, gifts, and talents because I am compelled to walk the way the Spirit guides. I believe that my needs and my heart's desires will be provided by God. Therefore, I will not lack or hoard. I expect God to keep His promises to provide abundantly.

MY PROVOKING THOUGHT OF THE DAY

The key difference between those who reach their full professional potential. and those who do not, is who they surround themselves with.

To be professionally successful, I need my own professional "Board of Directors." My board will push me when I need it. They will help me dream bigger than I can see, and they will invest their time and energy into helping me reach my destiny.

I trust my board with my professional well-being. I trust my board to help me develop and grow my professional skills and experience.

Who is on my board?

TODAY'S AFFIRMATION: DIALOGUING WITH GOD

Today, I dialogue with God about big things. I need help with my rent, but I ask to be blessed with my own home. I realize that God is moved by my faith. When I rely on him for all things big and small, it provides him the opportunity to show up in a big way in my life. I know He has plans to prosper and not harm me; so, I choose to prepare myself for God's prosperity. I realize asking God for things that are too big for me requires the faith in promises that only God can deliver. I come before the thrown boldly, knowing that God will provide all I ever ask, and even more than I can anticipate. I allow myself to think big today and to consider possibilities. What if I ran the department (or the company) instead of just working in it? What if I made straight A's in every class for the entire year? What if I started my own non-profit organization to help kids in education? What if I won a seat in the House of Representatives? Whatever vision God has planted in me, it is available to me; despite how impossible the vision may seem. What I know I can do does not require much faith, just effort. But, today, I am playing for something much bigger.

MY PROVOKING THOUGHT OF THE DAY

What if I chose to live completely free today? Free from ...

My past bad choices,
My past abuse,
My family deserting me,
My unhappy marriage,
and my dead end job.

What if I chose to immerse myself in complete joy? Joy that ...

I am alive,
I am powerful,
I am granted grace and mercy,
I am favored,
and I am desirable.

What if I chose to reinvent and redefine my life ... starting today?

TODAY'S AFFIRMATION: ACTING IN FAITH

The Gospel of Luke tells of the story of Simon Peter who was fishing at the Lake of Galilee. He had been fishing all night, but unable to catch any fish … nothing! Peter was an experienced fisherman, and had expertise in fishing. But, none of that mattered this day … he kept coming up empty. After Jesus taught the people from Peter's boat, Jesus told Peter to put his nets out in the deep water for a catch. Well, this sounded crazy! Peter had just been fishing all night and nothing was biting. Although dismayed, acting in faith and obedience, Peter put down the nets.

This is where the Gospel of Luke teaches me that acts of faith are richly rewarded. Peter's act of obedience yielded him so many fish, that he did not have room enough to receive. His nets began to break under the weight of all that fish; so, he had to call his partners over and all their boats were also filled to the point of sinking. Abundance involves overflow, but that overflow is not just for me. It is for those God has surrounded me with, who are also obedient. This is why abundant living does not covet; because there is no need to do so.

TODAY'S AFFIRMATION: CELEBRATING MY CIRCLE

Abundant living requires affirmation and celebration of those who are in my circle, not jealously. I ...

celebrate when my cousin gets a full scholarship,
even if I do not have one;
celebrate when my best friend gets engaged, even though I am not;
celebrate when my spouse gets a promotion,
even when I was passed over;
celebrate my neighbor's new car, even though mine is in the shop.

When I am connected to someone who is blessed, as they increase, so will I. The overflow of their blessing is coming my way. There is no need to compete with those in my circle. I do not have to take it from them or feel distressed. I am wary of those in my life, who do not uplift or celebrate me. Those who smirk at my success, downplay my blessings, and criticize my movements are blockers of my abundance. Those who exhibit these characteristics have a scarce mindset, which means they will never experience abundance themselves. Who is around me matters!

EXPOSURE

When God exposes me to something bigger or better or more productive; that opportunity is available to me.

If God places someone in my life, who inspires, motivates, and pushes me to my best; they are available to me.

If God exposes me to a professional opportunity that is a promotion over where I am today; it is available to me.

When God plants a vision about having children in my spirit; it is available to me.

The key to receive the blessing that is manifesting in my heart is to move with integrity and faith, and to prepare my heart and life to receive.

TODAY'S AFFIRMATION: AVIDLY GROWING

As an abundant consumer of knowledge, I am a voracious reader. Not required reading, such as reading for work or to help my kids with homework; but, I read to expand my mind and thinking. I read for information that shapes the world. I read for exposure to others' way of thinking, cultures, and experiences that may be different from my own. I read to enable my own imagination about my contribution to the world. I read books that challenge my beliefs, and that permit me to consider other ways of thinking. I read to be inspired by the others' stories. I read to expand my vocabulary, and my language capabilities. I read to learn about places and events that I have never experienced. I read to have clarity and context of my own history. I read to enable my ability to communicate with people in all parts of the world. I read as a quiet way to meditate, and to consider ideas and strategies. I read for my mind to explode with opportunities and possibilities. I read every day. The stronger my mind, the more confident my thoughts, the more impeccable my speech, and the more diverse are my actions. I read to cultivate the seed in me to grow to overflow!

BUT I GREW

The old me did not have the courage to try ... the new me walks in faith.

The old me did not have much to say ... the
new me values my own voice.

The old me was afraid to lose you ... the new me refuses to lose me.

The old me was content in mediocrity ... the new me is extraordinary.

The old me hid my pain ... the new me turns it into power.

The old me accepted your criticism ... the new me perseveres.

The old me dimmed my light behind you ...
the new me lets my light so shine.

The old me lacked self-esteem ... but I grew.

THE ICE CREAM MAN

Remember the ice cream man! It was the best feeling in the world to hear that little ice cream jingle. We did not have to see the truck, but we heard the jingle and knew that the ice cream was on the way. To receive the ice cream,

we grabbed our quarter;
put on our sneakers;
yelled to all our friends;
paused the kickball game; and
ran to the street, excitedly anticipating when
the ice cream truck would arrive.

While we were waiting, we talked about what type of ice cream we were going to buy and got in the best position on the right side of the street, so that the ice cream man could see us. It was nothing better when we got our Bomb Pop or Creamsicle or Nutty Buddy on a hot summer day!

THE SPIRITUAL ICE CREAM MAN

Well, this is how my abundant life with God works. I do not need to see what God is doing in my life; I just need to hear it. Upon hearing the Word that God has placed in my heart, I know the manifestation of that vision is on the way.

I grab my resources;
put on my whole armor of God;
yell to all my friends;
pause whatever I am engaged in my life and
run to the spot,
excitedly anticipating when my blessing will arrive.

While I am waiting, I speak the manifestation into my life, and I get in position to receive. I know that God will deliver the blessing; but, I can miss my opportunity if my heart is not on one accord with God. I know that waiting on the Lord is not a passive activity. I am in partnership with His Will for my life, and I commit to do my part. I know the pleasure of Gods refreshing anointing on my life on a hot summer's day is the best feeling in the world.

PAYING TITHES

Paying Tithes includes donating 10 percent of ...

My money to a church or a non-profit cause;

My energy to motivate others;

My time to help those less fortunate;

My expertise to mentor those coming behind me;

My health to invigorate and inspire others;

My opportunities to those without;

My love to those devoid of life;

My spirit of joy to those oppressed and depressed;

and my ideas to benefit the world.

TODAY'S AFFIRMATION: WAITING ON GOD

My abundant lifestyle understands that God has already done what He promised He would do in my life. There are times when He chooses to reveal my blessings in stages, based on my level of faith and readiness. However, "waiting on God" is not a passive activity. While waiting for the next steps in my journey to be revealed, I will prepare, and I make room for it.

If I am asking God for a new relationship, I may have to clear my heart and mind to make room for compromise and love.

If I am asking God to start a business, I may have to step out on faith and quit the old job, to make room for the business.

If I desire to volunteer at a non-profit, I may have to sacrifice my weekly night out with friends to make room in my schedule.

While I am waiting on God, maybe God is waiting on me.

TODAY'S AFFIRMATION:
SHARING MY GIFTS

Abundant thinkers share their time, energy, money, expertise, and everything else they have been gifted. This may seem counterintuitive, but I do not compete with others in any aspect of life ... professionally, personally, emotionally, or spiritually. I know that what God has for me is for me, and I understand that no one has the power to intercept the blessings God has destined for me (except me!). By its very nature, abundance requires the capacity to give.

I imagine trying to drink from a garden hose. When there is a kink in the hose (my blessings are blocked), water trickles out, often leaving me thirsty and barren. However, when my abundance is flowing freely, I cannot possibly drink all the water. I do not need to hoard water, because it is always flowing. Then I can take all the water I was unable to drink and I can overflow to quench the thirst of others. When I share the water of life, God increases the water pressure; more than I can possibly consume. No Room to Receive.

MY PROVOKING THOUGHT OF THE DAY

Who told us that love was supposed to be hard?

Who told us that love was about struggling in conflict?

Who told us that love was supposed to be mired in pain?

Who told us that love was about sticking in through abuse?

Who told us that love was supposed to be devaluing and dehumanizing?

Who told us that love was about getting … but not giving?

Who told us that love was supposed to hurt?

Love is … patient, kind, it does not envy or boast, it does not
dishonor others, is not angered or selfish, it forgives, is trustful, is
faithful, is humble, and is gentle, sincere, giving, and fearless …

What kind of love is this?

TODAY'S AFFIRMATION: CHALLENGING MYSELF

To maximize my life, I can never get too comfortable. If I strive to live abundantly, I must embrace change.

Challenging myself to become a better version of me requires me to relinquish the old version of me.

Challenging myself for more wisdom and vision requires me to shed what I thought I knew before.

Challenging myself for greater prosperity means I must be willing to risk what I currently have.

Challenging myself for promotion requires me to change my thinking from being a worker to being a manager.

Challenging myself for a great relationship requires me to reposition my mind from me to we.

Every new level God takes me will require a sacrifice. The unwillingness to change will leave me stuck in old ideas, old relationships, old experiences, and old situations leave me left behind.

TODAY'S AFFIRMATION:
GIFTED WITH BLESSINGS

I have been endowed with grace and favor. I have been gifted with blessings from God that I did not deserve and could not have earned. I live a life of gratitude for what I have been gifted; therefore, I show grace and favor to others. As I am blessed, I bless others.

I extend grace to those who have made bad choices;

I forgive those who have wronged me;

I endow favor on someone who needs a break;

And, I offer my best, even when I do not have to.

This is not about being taken advantage of. Abundant people know that rewards in this and the next life do not come from other people; but, rewards are gifted by God. Therefore, I feel compelled to spend a life of gratitude and giving. And, I watch how God shows out in mine.

TODAY'S AFFIRMATION: CRAZY FAITH

Faith will look crazy sometimes. It is ludicrous to quit a good job to start a business. It is bananas to go back to school at sixty-nine to get a master's degree. It is useless to try to write a book at sixteen years old. It seems foolish to turn down a sports scholarship to become a poet. However, I know that an abundant life will require some crazy decisions … a career change; the adoption of a teenager; trying to open a homeless shelter, with no money or shelter; or, leaving a 20-year relationship in which I was unfulfilled.

I know the definition of faith is the evidence of things not seen; so, many others will not see the vision God has planted in me. This means the moves I make will not be logical to them. By the way, along the journey, God will often place someone in my path who can see or understand my vision, and I will encourage me. I know if there is someone discouraging God's vision for my life, they are not sent by God. The enemy will use those who profess to love me to send doubt into my spirit, and to keep me nervous enough that I will not step out on faith.

PRAYER OF PEACE

Lord, I pray for peace ...

In my heart,
In my home,
In my life,
In my relationship,
For my children,
For my community,
For my family,
For my friends,
In my atmosphere,
In my country,
and In our world.

TODAY'S AFFIRMATION: NEGATIVE SELF-TALK

As an abundant thinker, I do not engage in negative self-talk. Self-reflection is necessary in the process of growth; however, self-criticism is not spiritual. Telling myself that ...

> I am not good enough;
> I am not smart enough;
> I won't ever make it; and
> I don't have what it takes

dishonors the grace God has given me. I strive to see myself the way God sees me. That means I do not hold my worst decisions and failures against me. I am made in God's image, which means I am built with power, strength, and grace. I trust God to stand in the gap of the things I cannot do, which enables me to do all things in Christ. I will not do the work of the enemy by talking myself out of opportunities, blessings, and growth. And, when I speak negative, I think negative, and I draw negative to me. I know that words have energy. When I change my perspective about what I have to offer, I offer something more valuable.

TODAY'S AFFIRMATION: DEFINING MY WORTH

I am exactly who God says I am. My worth is not defined by my job. I do not attach my worth to whether I am the supervisor or the worker. Positions change in life; however, I am always the head and not the tail. I do not attach my worth to how much money I make. There are times of financial prosperity and times of financial poverty; however, my needs will always be provided according to His riches in glory. I do not attach my worth to my spouse or significant other. I appreciate a person who also holds themselves to high value, who believes in me, and affirms me; but, I do not need them to create value in me. I am exactly who God says I am. I do not attach my value based on past decisions, good or bad. I am not the sum of my worst days or the product of my best. I continue to grow and learn every day, and I do not limit my value based on my previous self. I do not attach my value to how many designer possessions I own. I am exactly who God says I am, not who others think I am by the label on my body. When I am fully confident in my own self-worth, God will overflow that confidence to enable me to change the world around me. Then I will be exactly who God made me to be!

TODAY'S AFFIRMATION: ELIMINATING FEAR

Abundant livers do not fear failure. One of the greatest tricks of the enemy is to convince me not to try something for fear that it will not work. A great way to kill a vision is to kill it as a seed, before I try to materialize it. Abundance requires reimagining failure as something not to fear; but, something to embrace on the journey to destiny. Here is the thing about fear, it is not real! It is a construct that I create to cope with the feelings of disappointment.

As I walk in my calling, someone is going to dislike my efforts; I am going to be turned down for an opportunity I wanted; I am going to have to sacrifice some short-term financial goods for the long-term viability of my calling. However, these are not failures. They are just part of the process of birthing a vision. Morning sickness, kicking, hormonal changes, and labor pains are all part of the process. If I try to avoid the process, the miracle of birth never happens. Today, I embrace it.

MY PROVOKING THOUGHT OF THE DAY

Living a life with purpose ...

Is a life that is fulfilling;

Is a life that is expectant;

Is a life that is non-emotional;

Is a life that is mutable;

Is a life that endurable;

Is a life that is unshakable;

Is a life with a calling;

Is a life with resilience;

Is a life with resonance;

And, is a life with meaning.

What is my purpose?

TODAY'S AFFIRMATION: CULTIVATING MY SEED

I maximize what I have been given. God is not a respecter of persons, therefore, all of us have the same opportunity for happiness, health, love, and prosperity.

By the way, this does not diminish that we experience different circumstances in life …

some of us are born into wealth;
some of us are born into poverty;
some of us are born in a country with rights;
and, some of us are born with disadvantages.

However, I accept the premise that all of us are born with a seed. We each have the same opportunity to plant that seed, cultivate it, and use it to contribute something positive to the world.

God's grace stands in the gap of any disadvantages I think I have. I will use those circumstances to make me more powerful, and to make a bigger impact.

TODAY'S AFFIRMATION: FULFILLING MY PURPOSE

I will not be distracted by things that keep me from fulfilling my purpose. I will not spend my life existing, working, but being woefully unhappy. To fulfill my purpose, I have to first seek it, try to understand it, foster, and to develop it. I know that my purpose and calling is always presented as a seed. I must plant the seed, water it, and fertilize it to bears fruit. Then, I can collect the harvest, which abounds for myself and overflow to others.

Purpose requires self-reflection and dedication, seeking revelation.

God will reveal my purpose, and the resources He has already provided for that purpose to come to fruition. When I live a life of purpose, abundance flows through my life, including joy, health, and richness. I will not block my blessings by being distracted by the shiny objects of the enemy … like my job, a relationship, and material possessions.

TODAY'S AFFIRMATION: REPLACING A BACKUP PLAN

As an abundant consumer of life, I am rethinking what I have been taught about having a fallback plan. A fallback plan is a plan in my back pocket, for when my dream does not work out. The more I think about it, a backup plan can stunt my faith. When God plants a dream or vision in my life, my job is to believe in that vision, and to be faithful until it materializes. I now believe the backup plan gives me an out to believing in God's plan, and to living in expectation for God to deliver.

I replace the fallback plan with the "on the way" plan. Along the journey to realization, I may take interim steps; but, I am clear how each step is moving me toward that vision. A job to pay the bills, while perfecting my craft is not a backup plan; it is a step closer. Taking a few classes at night to increase my knowledge, while I am writing my book is not a backup plan; it is a step closer. Being an understudy in the play, while observing the lead is not a backup plan; it is a step closer. Along the way, I never give up on my vision and I stay expectant and prepared for God to work in my life.

TODAY'S AFFIRMATION: FACING PROBLEMS

Although I aspire to an abundant life, I do not avoid problems. I have courage to confront the process and grow through it. It requires deliberation to deal with some of the circumstances I will experience. But, I trust and have confidence in my ability to overcome them. I approach tough circumstances with grace, and I recognize there are times when life will throw me difficult situations. I know that strong minds do not crumble, and I accept these valleys as part of my life experience.

Abundant living does not mean I get a pass to negative experiences. But, I know that I can fear no evil knowing that God is with me; although, I may have to walk through some dark times. I resist taking a seasonal problem and making it a lifetime one. A new season is bound to come.

TODAY'S AFFIRMATION: LIVING TRANSPARENTLY

I do not define myself by whether I am an introvert or an extrovert ... that is about personality. I understand that my life is designed to be a positive example to other people about the fullness and the bigness of God. Therefore, I accept responsibility of living life in a positive, affirming way. I have gratitude that God uses my life, my circumstances, and my experiences to encourage and motivate others to overcome. I acknowledge the power in being vulnerable enough to let my life be an example. It requires an openness and transparency to share my life experiences, as a testimony to what is possible. Therefore, I embrace my flaws, poor choices and bad experiences as growth moments to demonstrate grace. I know that holding on to the shame and the pain of my past blocks abundance, and it keeps me mired in discontent and negative energy. I choose to live abundantly and not in lack.

PRAYER OF PROSPERITY

Father God, thank You for the abundant life you've promised, and have already delivered for me. Thank You for providing all my needs according to Your riches in glory. Thank You for giving me all that I need, and overflowing my life with the fruits of the Spirit. Thank You for overflowing my anointing to help those around me. Thank You for overflowing my oil jars to spread love around the world. Thank You for overflowing my resources to help the least of these. Thank You for overflowing my love to embrace and love all those I encounter. Thank You for overflowing my strength and passion to run life's race. Thank You for prospering me in such an abundant way, that I don't have room enough to receive.

THE BIBLICAL SCRIPTURES FROM
THE KING JAMES VERSION

But my God shall supply all your need according to His riches in glory by Christ Jesus. Philippians 4:19

For I know the thoughts that I think toward you, saith the Lord, thoughts of peace and not of evil to give you an expected end. Then shall ye call upon me, and ye shall go and pray unto me, and I will hearken unto you. Jeremiah 29:11-12

Beloved, I wish above all things that thou mayest prosper and be in health, even as they soul prospereth. 3 John 2:2

And God is able to make grace abound toward you, that ye, always having all sufficiency in all things, may abound to every good work. 2 Corinthians 9:8

And He shall be like a tree planted by the rivers of water, that bringeth forth His fruit in His season; His leaf shall not wither; and whatsoever He doeth shall prosper. Psalm 1:3

Give and it shall be given unto you; good measure, pressed down, and shaken together; and running over; shall men given into your bosom. For the same measure that ye mete withal it shall be measured to you again. Luke 6:38

Praise ye the Lord. Blessed is the man that feareth the Lord, that delighteth greatly in His commandments. His seed shall be mighty upon earth; the generation of the upright shall be blessed. Wealth and riches shall be in His house; and His righteousness endureth forever. Psalms 112:1-3

THE BIBLICAL SCRIPTURES FROM
THE KING JAMES VERSION

Now until him that is able to do exceedingly abundantly above all that we ask or think, according to the power that worketh in us. Ephesians 3:20

Thou preparest a table before me in the presence of mine enemies; thou annointest my head with oil; my cup runneth over. Psalm 23:5

The thief cometh not, but for to steal, and to kill, and to destroy; I am come that they might have life, and that they might have it more abundantly. John 10:10

But seek ye first the kingdom of God, and His righteousness; and all these things shall be added unto you. Matthew 6:33

But the meek shall inherit the earth; and shall delight themselves in the abundance of peace. Psalms 37:11

Now the God of hope fill you with all joy and peace in believing, that ye may abound in hope, through the power of the Holy Ghost. Romans 15:13

I can do all things through Christ which strengthen me. Philippians 4:13

Blessed is the man that walketh not in the counsel of the ungodly, nor standeth in the way of sinners, or sitteth in the seat of scornful. But His delight is in the law of the Lord, and in His law doth He meditate day and night. And He shall be like a tree planted by the rivers of waters, that bringeth forth His fruit in His season, His leaf shall not wither, and whatsoever He doeth shall prosper. Psalm 1:1-3

THE BIBLICAL SCRIPTURES FROM
THE KING JAMES VERSION

For God hath not given us the spirit of fear; but of power, and of love, and of a sound mind. 2 Timothy 1:7

Be careful for nothing; but in everything by prayer and supplication with thanksgiving let your requests be made known unto God. Philippians 4:6

Simon Peter saith unto them, I go a fishing. They said unto him, we also go with thee. They went forth, and entered into a ship immediately, and that night they caught nothing ... And He said unto them, Cast the net on the right side of the ship and ye shall find. They cast therefore, and now they were not able to draw it for the multitude of fishes. And the other disciplines came in a little ship, dragging the net with fishes. Simon Peter went up, and drew the net to land full of great fishes, and hundred and fifty and three; and for all there were so many, yet was not the net broken. John 21:3, 6, 8, 11.

The Lord is my light and my salvation; whom shall I fear? The Lord is the strength of my life; of whom shall I be afraid. Psalm 27:1

Ask, and it shall be given you; seek, and Ye shall find; knock, and it shall be opened unto you: For every one that asketh receiveth; and He that seeketh findeth, and to him that knocketh it shall be opened. Matthew 7:7-8

And the Lord answered me, and said, Write the vision and make it plain upon tables, that He may run that readeth it. For the vision is yet for an appointed time, but at the end it shall speak, and not lie: though it tarry, wait for it; because it will surely come, it will not tarry. Habakkuk 2:2-3

For we walk by faith, not by sight. 2 Corinthians 5:7

THE BIBLICAL SCRIPTURES FROM
THE KING JAMES VERSION

But without faith it is impossible to please him; for He that cometh to God must believe that He is, and that he is a rewarder of them that diligently seek him. Hebrews 11:6

So then faith cometh by hearing, and hearing by the word of God. Romans 10:17

Now faith is the substance of things hoped for, the evidence of things not seen. Hebrews 11:1

Jesus said unto him, if thou canst believe, all things are possible to him that believeth. Mark 9:23

For verily I say unto you, that whosoever shall say unto this mountain, Be thou removed, and be thou cast into the sea; and shall not doubt in His heart, but shall believe that those things which He saith shall come to pass; He shall have whatsoever He saith. Mark 11:23

Let your light so shine before men, that they may see your good works, and glorify your Father which is in heaven. Matthew 5:16

And this the confidence that we have in him, that, if we ask any thing according to His well, He heareth us. 1 John 5:14

For the love of money is the root of all evil; which while some coveted after, they have erred from the faith, and pierced themselves through with many sorrows. 1 Timothy 6:10

THE BIBLICAL SCRIPTURES FROM
THE KING JAMES VERSION

Wealth gotten by vanity shall be diminished; but He that gathereth by labour shall increase. Proverbs 13:11

Charge them that are rich in this world, that they be not highminded, nor trust in uncertain riches, but in the living God, who giveth us richly all things to enjoy. That they do good, that they be rich in good works, ready to distribute, willing to communicate. 1 Timothy 6:17-18

Honour the Lord with thy substance and with the first fruits of all thine increase. So shall thy barns be filled with plenty, and thy presses shall burst out with new wine. Proverbs 3:9-10

The wicket borroweth, and payeth not again, but the righteous sheweth mercy, and giveth. Psalm 37:21

And the King shall answer and say unto them, Verily I say unto you, inasmuch as ye have done it unto one of the least of these my brethren, ye have done it unto me. Matthew 25: 40

And we know that all things work together for good to them that love God, to them who are called according to His purpose. Romans 8:28

Ye have not chosen me, but I have chosen you, and ordained you, that ye should go and bring forth fruit, and that your fruit should remain: that whatsoever ye shall ask of the Father in my name, He may give it to you. John 15:16

THE BIBLICAL SCRIPTURES FROM
THE KING JAMES VERSION

In whom also we have obtained an inheritance, being predestinated according to the purpose of him who worketh all things after the counsel of His own will. Ephesians 1:11

Who hath saved us, and called us with a holy calling, not according to our works, but according to His own purpose and grace, which was given us in Christ Jesus before the world began. 2 Timothy 1:9

For many are called, but few are chosen. Matthew 22:14

Call unto me, and I will answer thee, and shew thee great and mighty things which though knowest not. Jeremiah 33:3

For every good gift and every perfect gift is from above, and cometh down from the Father of lights, with whom there is no variableness, neither shadow of turning. James 1:19

For the gifts and calling of God are without repentance. Romans 11:29

Be not deceived; God is not mocked; for whatsoever a man soweth, that shall He also reap. Galatians 6:7

But this I say, He which soweth sparingly shall reap also sparingly; and He which soweth bountifully shall reap also bountifully. 2 Corinthians 9:6

But the fruit of the spirit is love, joy, peace, longsuffering, gentleness, goodness, faith, meekness temperance: against such there is no law. Galatians 5:22-23

THE BIBLICAL SCRIPTURES FROM THE KING JAMES VERSION

Delight thyself also in the Lord; and He shall give thee the desires of thine heart. Psalms 37:4

For there is no respect of persons with God. Romans 2:11

And also that every man should eat and drink, and enjoy the good of all His labour, it is the gift of God. Ecclesiastes 3:13

Thou will keep him in perfect peace, whose mind is stayed on thee: because He trusteth in thee. Isaiah 26:3

Blessed be the Lord, who daily loadeth us with benefits, even the God of our salvation. Selah. Psalms 68:19

What time I am afraid, I will trust in thee. In God I will praise His word, in God I have put my trust; I will not fear what flesh can do unto me. Psalm 56: 3-4

There is no fear in love; but perfect love casteth out fear; because fear hath torment. He that feareth is not made perfect in love. 1 John 4:18

Commit thy works unto the Lord, and they thoughts shall be established. Proverbs 16:3

And be not conformed to this world, but be ye transformed by the renewing of your mind, that ye may prove what is that good, and acceptable, and perfect, will of God. Romans 12:2

THE BIBLICAL SCRIPTURES FROM
THE KING JAMES VERSION

But know that the Lord hath set apart him that is godly for himself; the Lord will hear when I call unto him. Psalm 4:3

And now abideth faith, hope, charity, these three; but the greatest of these is charity. 1 Corinthians 13:13

And all things, whatsoever ye shall ask in prayer, believing, ye shall receive. Matthew 21:22

And the Lord shall guide thee continually, and satisfy thy soul in drought, and make fat thy bones; and thou shalt be like a watered garden, and like a spring of water, whose waters fail not. Isaiah 58:11

Behold that which I have seen; it is good and comely for one to eat and to drink and to enjoy the good of all His labour that He taketh under the sun of the days of His life, which God giveth him; for it is His portion. Ecclesiastes 5:18

The Story of Jesus feeding the thousands with fish and bread: Matthew 14: 13-21

And He said unto them, Take Heed and beware of covetousness; for a man's life consisteth not in the abundance of the things which He possesses. Luke 12:15

Ye are of God, little children, and have overcome them; because greater is He that is in you, than He that is in the world. 1 John 4:4

THE BIBLICAL SCRIPTURES FROM
THE KING JAMES VERSION

And Jesus said unto them, Because of your unbelief; for verily I say unto you, if you have faith as a grain of a mustard seed, ye shall say unto this mountain, remove hence to yonder place; and it shall remove; and nothing shall be impossible unto you. Matthew 17:20

And the LORD shall make thee the head, and not the tail; and thou shalt be above only, and thou shall not be beneath, if thou hearken unto the commandments of the Lord thy God which I command thee this day, to observe and to do them. Deuteronomy 28:13

But He that knew not and committed things worthy of stripes, shall be beaten with few stripes. For unto whomsoever much His given, of him shall much be required; and to whom men have committed much, of him will they ask the more. Luke 12:48

But I say unto you, Love your enemies, bless them that curse you, do good to them that hate you, and pray for them which despitefully use you, and persecute you. Matthew 5:44

That ye may be the children of your Father which is in heaven; for He maketh His sun to rise on the evil and on the good, and sendeth rain on the just and on the unjust. Matthew 5:45

For our light affliction, which is but for a moment, worketh for us a far more exceeding and eternal weight of glory; While we look not at the things which are seen, but at the things which are not seen: for the things which are seen are temporal; but the things which are not seen are eternal. 2 Corinthians 4:17-18

THE BIBLICAL SCRIPTURES FROM THE KING JAMES VERSION

No weapon that is formed against thee shall prosper; and every tongue that shall rise against thee in judgment thou shall condemn. This is the heritage of the servants of the Lord, and their righteousness is of me, saith the Lord. Isaiah 54:17

Whoso sheddeth man's blood, By man His blood shall be shed; For in the image of God He made man. Genesis 9:6

Therefore I say unto you, What things soever ye desire, when ye pray, believe that ye receive them, and ye shall have them. Mark 11:24

There is that scattereth, and yet increaseth; and there is that withholdeth more than is meet, but it tendeth to poverty. Proverbs 11:24

Every good gift and every perfect gift is from above, and cometh down from the Father of lights, with whom is no variableness, neither shadow of turning. James 1:17

For the love of money is the root of all evil; which while some coveted after, they have erred from the faith, and pierced themselves through with many sorrows. 1 Timothy 6:10

What shall we than say to these things? If God be for us, who can be against us? Romans 8:31

The thief cometh not, but for to steal, and to kill, and to destroy; I am come that they might have life, and that they might have it more abundantly. John 10:10

THE BIBLICAL SCRIPTURES FROM
THE KING JAMES VERSION

Let your conversation be without covetousness; and be content with such things as ye have: for He hath said, I will never leave thee, nor forsake thee. Hebrews 13:5

AUTHOR'S PAGE

Anita D. Powell, Esq is proud to present her first published work. She is a powerful woman of God, with a passion to motivate, encourage and inspire the world to the glory of God.

Anita holds a Bachelor of Science (BS) degree in Electrical Engineering from Hampton University, a Juris Doctor (JD) in Employment and Labor Law from Temple University, and is currently a Doctor of Philosophy (PhD) student at Liberty University, studying Industrial and Organizational Psychology.

Anita is the Owner and Principal Consultant of the Employee and Labor Relations Academy, a business consulting firm specializing in employment law matters. She is also the Owner of 1Nterprises, LLC, and engages as a motivational speaker and writer. Anita also founded and runs the JWP foundation, which is a non-profit foundation designed to eradicate homelessness and food insecurity.

Anita is blessed to have one amazing son, Worthy, and a host of wonderful family and friends. She lives in the DC Metro Area.

A SPECIAL THANK YOU ...

To all of the many spiritual leaders and advisers who have contributed to my spiritual growth over the course of my life. I am thankful to Mom and Dad, who introduced me to Christ at a very young age. To the wonderful Pastors and Teachers who have shared wisdom and a contagious spirit that have contributed to my spiritual discipline. I am grateful to my family and friends for supporting this project and receiving and believing in my growth. Having a village of support makes all the difference.

DEDICATION

*To my son Worthy, who inspires and teaches me to
live at the very top of my life every day.*

Printed in the USA
CPSIA information can be obtained
at www.ICGtesting.com
LVHW052340220823
756019LV00013BA/45/J